MACMILLAN MODI

General Editor: N

MACMILLAN MODERN NOVELISTS

Published titles
MARGARET ATWOOD Coral Ann Howells
SAUL BELLOW Peter Hyland
ALBERT CAMUS Philip Thody
FYODOR DOSTOEVSKY Peter Conradi
GEORGE ELIOT Alan W. Bellringer
WILLIAM FAULKNER David Dowling
GUSTAVE FLAUBERT David Roe
E. M. FORSTER Norman Page
ANDRÉ GIDE David Walker
WILLIAM GOLDING James Gindin
GRAHAM GREENE Neil McEwan
ERNEST HEMINGWAY Peter Messent
CHRISTOPHER ISHERWOOD Stephen Wade
HENRY JAMES Alan W. Bellringer
JAMES JOYCE Richard Brown
D. H. LAWRENCE G. M. Hyde
ROSAMOND LEHMANN Judy Simons
DORIS LESSING Ruth Whittaker
MALCOLM LOWRY Tony Bareham
NORMAN MAILER Michael K. Glenday
THOMAS MANN Martin Travers
GABRIEL GARCÍA MÁRQUEZ Michael Bell
TONI MORRISON Linden Peach
IRIS MURDOCH Hilda D. Spear
VLADIMIR NABOKOV David Rampton
V. S. NAIPAUL Bruce King
GEORGE ORWELL Valerie Meyers
ANTHONY POWELL Neil McEwan
MARCEL PROUST Philip Thody
BARBARA PYM Michael Costell
JEAN-PAUL SARTRE Philip Thody
SIX WOMEN NOVELISTS Merryn Williams
MURIEL SPARK Norman Page
JOHN UPDIKE Judie Newman
EVELYN WAUGH Jacqueline McDonnell
H. G. WELLS Michael Draper
VIRGINIA WOOLF Edward Bishop
PATRICK WHITE Mark Williams

Forthcoming titles
SIMONE DE BEAUVOIR Terry Keefe
IVY COMPTON-BURNETT Janet Godden
JOSEPH CONRAD Owen Knowles
JOHN FOWLES James Acheson
FRANZ KAFKA Ronald Spiers and Beatrice Sandberg
SALMAN RUSHDIE D. C. R. A. Goonetilleke
MARK TWAIN Peter Messent
ALICE WALKER Maria Lauret

MACMILLAN MODERN NOVELISTS
NORMAN MAILER

Michael K. Glenday

© Michael K. Glenday 1995

All rights reserved. No reproduction, copy or transmission of this publication may be made without written permission.

No paragraph of this publication may be reproduced, copied or transmitted save with written permission or in accordance with the provisions of the Copyright, Designs and Patents Act 1988, or under the terms of any licence permitting limited copying issued by the Copyright Licensing Agency, 90 Tottenham Court Road, London W1P 9HE.

Any person who does any unauthorised act in relation to this publication may be liable to criminal prosecution and civil claims for damages.

First published 1995 by
MACMILLAN PRESS LTD
Houndmills, Basingstoke, Hampshire RG21 2XS
and London
Companies and representatives
throughout the world

ISBN 0-333-52261-3 hardcover
ISBN 0-333-52262-1 paperback

10 9 8 7 6 5 4 3 2 1
04 03 02 01 00 99 98 97 96 95

A catalogue record for this book is available
from the British Library.

Typeset by Nick Allen/Longworth Editorial Services
Longworth, Oxfordshire.

Printed in Malaysia

Series Standing Order
If you would like to receive future titles in this series as they are published, you can make use of our standing order facility. To place a standing order, please contact your bookseller or, in case of difficulty, write to us at the address below with your name and address and the name of the series. Please state with which title you wish to begin your standing order. (If you live outside the United Kingdom we may not have the rights for your area, in which case we will forward your order to the publisher concerned.)

Customer Services Department, Macmillan Distribution Ltd
Houndmills, Basingstoke, Hampshire, RG 21 2XS, England.

For Jas

Artists embodied the essence of what was best in the nation, embodied it in their talent rather than in their character, which could be small.

      Norman Mailer, *The Presidential Papers*

America – his country. An empty country filled with wonders.

      Norman Mailer, *Of a Fire on the Moon*

Contents

	Acknowledgements	viii
	General Editor's Preface	ix
1	Introduction: The Shaping of Personality	1
2	The Hot Breath of the Future: *The Naked and the Dead*	46
3	Ambush in the Alley: *Barbary Shore* and *The Deer Park*	62
4	A Plunge into the Age: *An American Dream* and *Why Are We in Vietnam?*	84
5	From Egypt to Langley: *Ancient Evenings, Tough Guys Don't Dance* and *Harlot's Ghost*	115
	Notes	144
	Select Bibliography	158
	Index	162

Acknowledgements

I gratefully acknowledge the financial assistance of the University of Liverpool Board of College Studies which awarded me a Research Grant for this study. I am also grateful to the Liverpool Institute of Higher Education for a period of study leave. Thanks are also due to the Library of LIHE, and particularly to the Inter-Library Loans staff for their efficient assistance in obtaining research material. In the Department of American Studies at LIHE, I am grateful to Gail Redmond for her secretarial assistance. I acknowledge a general debt to my colleagues and students, and it is a pleasure to have this opportunity to thank my colleague Dr William Blazek, who read several chapters of the work with the keenest eye. For his generous interest in the project I am most grateful.

General Editor's Preface

The death of the novel has often been announced, and part of the secret of its obstinate vitality must be its capacity for growth, adaptation, self-renewal and self-transformation: like some vigorous organism in a speeded-up Darwinian ecosystem, it adapts itself quickly to a changing world. War and revolution, economic crisis and social change, radically new ideologies such as Marxism and Freudianism, have made this century unprecedented in human history in the speed and extent of change, but the novel has shown an extraordinary capacity to find new forms and techniques and to accommodate new ideas and conceptions of human nature and human experience, and even to take up new positions on the nature of fiction itself.

In the generations immediately preceding and following 1914, the novel underwent a radical redefinition of its nature and possibilities. The present series of monographs is devoted to the novelists who created the modern novel and to those who, in their turn, either continued and extended, or reacted against and rejected, the traditions established during that period of intense exploration and experiment. It includes a number of those who lived and wrote in the nineteenth century but whose innovative contribution to the art of fiction makes it impossible to ignore them in any account of the origins of the modern novel; it also includes the so-called 'modernists' and those who in the mid- and late twentieth century have merged as outstanding practitioners of this genre. The scope is, inevitably, international; not only, in the migratory and exile-haunted world of our century, do writers refuse to heed national frontiers – 'English' literature lays claim to Conrad the Pole, Henry James the American, and Joyce the Irishman – but geniuses such as Flaubert, Dostoevsky and Kafka have had an influence on the fiction of many nations.

Each volume in the series is intended to provide an introduction to the fiction of the writer concerned, both for those approaching him or her for the first time and for those who are already familiar with some parts of the achievement in question and now wish to place it in the context of the total *oeuvre*. Although essential information relating to the writer's life and times is given, usually in an opening chapter, the approach is primarily critical and the emphasis is not upon 'background' or generalisations but upon close examination of important texts. Where an author is notably prolific, major texts have been made to convey, more summarily, a sense of the nature and quality of the author's work as a whole. Those who want to read further will find suggestions in the select bibliography included in each volume. Many novelists are, of course, not only novelists but also poets, essayists, biographers, dramatists, travel writers and so forth; many have practised shorter forms of fiction; and many have written letters or kept diaries that constitute a significant part of their literary output. A brief study cannot hope to deal with all these in detail, but where the shorter fiction and the non-fictional writings, public and private, have an important relationship to the novels, some space has been devoted to them.

NORMAN PAGE

1
Introduction: The Shaping of Personality

In a piece of middlebrow mischief, the *Guardian* newspaper recently awarded Norman Mailer his latest title, that of 'greatest literary bore of the 20th century'.[1] The anonymous columnist considered that Mailer had been challenged very closely by two other Americans, Henry James and Ernest Hemingway, but that finally Mailer's ability to bore his readers was without true rival. 'While critics have remained respectful the public is beginning to rumble Mailer. His latest book, *Harlot's Ghost*, sold very poorly indeed.'[2] I offer this more as an instance of Mailer's enduring ability to remain situated provocatively in public view than as any ultimate judgement. Yet it would be irony indeed if Mailer – once dubbed 'the Bore Buster' by journalists following his New York City mayoralty campaign in 1969[3] – could now be dismissed as a writer on the tedious margins. Perhaps in England particularly, his grandstanding approach has fitted all too easily into a stereotype of ugly Americanism. Yet by refusing the quietism and mannered detachment of the old-time writer, Mailer also prepared himself for the emerging culture of postmodernism. 'The first art work in an artist is the shaping of his own personality'[4] would soon be his conviction, and more than any writer of his age his personality was a radical element in the cultural battlegrounds of America in the postwar years. For Mailer, personality would be one crucial weapon in the struggle to matter, to intervene in the age. As Richard Gilman remarked of him, he was prepared to 'go to the end, to the other side of personality and coherent being, to be *pertinent*, literally to figure in'[5] the making of cultural history.

As a young student of aeronautical engineering at Harvard in the early 1940s, Mailer did strike some who knew him as 'a bore', because he insisted they acknowledge his cultural origins – 'everybody found him boring because he spent most of his time claiming that he was just a poor Jewish boy from Brooklyn'.[6] In later years he consciously refused the security of typecasting himself as anything so singular, preferring instead a fluidity of persona, a protean self very much in keeping with his later self-definition as an American existentialist. 'I suppose there are two recurring subjects in my life that just fascinate me over and over again. One of them is the establishment. The other is identity.'[7] Mailer might have added that the relationship between the two subjects has also been an abiding fascination for him, as for so many fellow Americans writing in the years since 1945. Certainly his own career as a writer has been rightly described as 'a personal index of American history since the Second World War',[8] a career styled by diversity, unpredictability, and an unfailingly bold approach to his great and epic subject: American reality in all its concern with the embattled relationship between individualism and power.

'I think he's our greatest writer. And what is unfortunate is our greatest writer should be a bum.'[9] So wrote Pauline Kael of Norman Mailer, echoing the judgement of Richard Poirier who, a year earlier in 1972 had also remarked the central contradiction in him: 'on the one hand the marvellously fastidious stylist, a writer almost precious in his care for phrasing and cadence, and, on the other and seemingly at odds, the boisterous, the vulgar actor'.[10] These roles were ones present from college days; when confronted by the Harvard establishment, the Harvard *Advocate* staffers, Mailer began to fashion one of his most notorious personas, ' a sort of literary tough guy, something like a Hemingway knock-off'[11] as one of his Harvard roommates remembered. Though the two men never met, Hemingway would later describe Mailer as:

> probably the best postwar writer. He's a psycho, but the psy-

Introduction: The Shaping of Personality

cho part is the most interesting thing about him. Chances are he won't be able to throw another fit like *The Naked and the Dead*. But if he does . . . I better watch out.[12]

The two writers are often compared, yet beyond superficial similarities they are separated by more profound differences. As one critic remarked, 'unlike Hemingway with his one-man style, Mailer has turned into an everyman'.[13] Mailer's sub-Hemingway persona was to become only one part of a quick-changing repertoire of contemporary address.

Yet anyone attempting a fix on Mailer's life and career will soon enough confront a further paradox – that for all his public exposure, his life as one of the very few writers of distinction to have also existed as a celebrity, his private life, apart from a few lurid incidents, has escaped the media spotlight. He has shown skill in achieving celebrity for his ideas, dramatising the public personae, while remaining essentially private. According to Alfred Kazin, Mailer has 'an ability to make his imagination public. One somehow knew not Mailer himself . . . but Mailer's fetishes, his drive, his necessary plunge into events, his ability to make connections between his psyche and American life.'[14] Even while a young student at Harvard, Mailer was regarded as in control of his private as much as his public personality:

> He was a self-defined loner. . . . He was training himself quite explicitly, and anyone who knew him thought of him as *sui generis*, always an individual with a sense of mission. He was thought of as exceptional but too controlled, *too* disciplined. . . . He was an enigma. He had a secret life in the sense that you knew only so much about him and there was an aura you couldn't penetrate.[15]

Mailer's self-discipline, his commitment to a career as a writer, was evident at an early age. His aspirations were encouraged by his parents. As he remembers, 'I didn't have to convince my parents that I should be a writer. . . . They were soon pleased that I wanted to be a writer. They loved reading my work, as only parents can.'[16] He wrote what he called his 'first half-decent story' in the summer of 1940, while on vacation after his first year at Harvard.

Mailer is the only son of a second-generation immigrant family, and by far the most significant influence in his early years was that of his mother, by all accounts a dominating personality who believed fiercely in her son's abilities:

> Two formative currents of personality came together to make my nature. . . . One of them is being Jewish. I'm not a Holocaust hustler, I'm not asking for pity, but every Jew alive feels his relationship to the world is somehow more tenuous than other people's, and so to affirm his existence is somehow more important. The second current was that I had a mother who spoiled me out of sight, with all that's good and bad about that, so I was accustomed to having attention paid to me, and that is probably the key to my personality.[17]

Fanny Mailer 'completely took over' in the domestic scene and 'nursed all of Norman's narcissism, and made him feel that whatever he did was okay'.[18] In comparison the father, Isaac Barnett (Barney) Mailer was a minor influence. Mailer was named Nachum Malech, his middle name meaning 'king' in Hebrew. Although this was subsequently altered to 'Kingsley', for Fanny Mailer the original choice was more meaningful, for to her and her family, 'that's what he was, our little king . . . he was like a little god'.[19] This 'terribly tough, strong woman' instilled in her son an unshakeable sense of his having a special destiny, even though – perhaps unsurprisingly – this had to wait until after he had left home to acquire a specific shape. When Mailer failed on one occasion to achieve the expected 'A' grade on one of his school report cards (though he later made up for the lapse, graduating from the Boys High School in Brooklyn with an IQ of 165, this being what his school principal called 'the highest IQ we've ever had'),[20] Fanny Mailer rushed to the principal, demanding that the grade be changed to an 'A' on the grounds that Norman was 'a superior person'. The offending teacher was remembered by Fanny Mailer as 'a big fat Irishwoman' who had failed to recognise that if Mailer 'didn't pay

Introduction: The Shaping of Personality

attention' in her class 'it was because he already knew it all'.[21] Under this kind of matriarchal influence, it may not surprise that Mailer is best remembered by his boyhood friends for being 'on a shorter leash, more obedient, kind of quiet'[22] compared to them, and for spending most of his free time building model airplanes. Mailer, for his part, returned the mother's devotion throughout his life, a fact remembered somewhat ruefully by Lady Jeanne Campbell, his third wife. After their separation, she remarked, 'here I married this terrific, powerful, dynamic, romantic literary man, and he turned out to be a guy who had to go see his mother every Friday night for dinner'.[23]

Of the two 'formative currents' of his personality noted above, Mailer's acknowledgement of the Jewish influence is the more problematical. His maternal grandfather was a Talmudic scholar who, though without his own congregation, was regarded as the unofficial rabbi of his locality of Long Branch, New Jersey. Yet though he was born into a very Jewish community, and appeared sensitive to his Jewish origins while at Harvard, his work (with the exception of *The Naked and the Dead*, which exposes the anti-Semitic bigotry aimed at characters such as Roth and Goldstein) shows few explicit signs of a self-conscious Jewish sensibility at work. In an interview of 1963, he admitted that his 'knowledge of Jewish culture is exceptionally spotty',[24] and for some of his Jewish contemporaries, such as Norman Podhoretz, Mailer's relationship to Jewishness remains problematical:

> That a man of his curiosity and energy should show so little interest about something so close to him, something that is in his blood, is extraordinary. Just the fact that he's never gone to Israel is in itself suspicious.[25]

Yet it is possible also to see Mailer as most Jewish even in this apparent rejection of traditional ties. For Alfred Kazin, Mailer belongs rather to another Jewish tradition, that of radical individualism:

> Jewishness Mailer disliked because it limited and intellectualized. . . . With his contempt for knowledge-as-control, his

desire to leave all those centuries of Jewish tradition (and of Jewish losers) behind him, Mailer represents the unresting effort and overreaching of the individual Jewish writer who seeks to be nothing but an individual (and if possible a hero).[26]

Mailer, then, perpetuates a line of Jewish individualism of which his rabbi grandfather would have approved, for he was the unofficial rabbi who 'never wanted a congregation because he said that rabbis were *schnorrers* and he wouldn't live that way'.[27]

Mailer is one of the most politically engaged writers to have emerged in the United States after the Second World War, and one of his greatest achievements is to have translated political crisis into moral and spiritual terms. His first two novels, *The Naked and the Dead* (1948) and *Barbary Shore* (1951), reveal a vision of the world which assumes the awesome march of political power, be it fascism, totalitarianism or Stalinism. In his anthology *Advertisements for Myself* (1959) and the novel *An American Dream* (1965), we see him fashioning his own idiosyncratic response to American politics, advocating in his famous essay 'The White Negro' a new form of existential heroism mediated through violent dissent. Together with his political journalism – his 'informal histories' of American political conventions such as those taking place in 1968 and published as *Miami and the Siege of Chicago* – these are the writings to be foregrounded in a life of political radicalism and vision. Indeed Norman Podhoretz saw Mailer, along with Paul Goodman and Norman O. Brown, as one of this trio of 'prophets' who ensured 'that the radicalism of the sixties was born'.[28]

In his first novel, politics are embodied in a group of main characters, in the struggle between the liberal Lieutenant Hearn, the sado-fascistic General Cummings and the similarly drawn Sergeant Croft. The novel's climax sees Hearn effectively murdered by Croft, and both Croft and Cummings reduced by the triumph of the military bureaucracy, itself a version of the totalitarianism which Mailer saw as already widespread throughout American society. The novel's political plot and Mailer's concerns about American politics are closely linked. Since the late

Introduction: The Shaping of Personality 7

1940s, his politics have travelled along the spectrum from far left to right, but in those early years his Marxist sympathies were unequivocal. While in Paris where he had been staying with his first wife, Bea, just prior to the publication of *The Naked and the Dead*, Mailer had met Jean Malaquais, who became something of a mentor in his political education. Although Malaquais was attracted by the intellectual energy of the young Mailer, he also saw him as 'naive, a kind of Boy Scout intellectually and politically'.[29] Malaquais was a Polish immigrant who occupied a position on the enlightened left; in common with many other writers and artists in Europe and America, he had repudiated Stalinism after the Moscow show-trials. He was not only a political sophisticate but had already expressed his politics artistically in the novels *World without Visa* and *The Man From Nowhere*, which had won him the prestigious Prix Renaudot. With Malaquais to guide him, Mailer quickly came to regard political engagement as a *raison d'écrire*. As Hilary Mills notes, 'Mailer had ... adopted the European idea that a writer does not exist in a vacuum.'[30] Mills is right, but Mailer had already absorbed an earlier influence which saw art as politically rooted. While at Harvard he had been exposed to a leftist intellectual model in the form of the first American Studies programme, initiated by the great Americanist, F. O. Mathiessen:

> Begun at Harvard ... and already gaining acceptance at other universities, the program emphasised that literature should not be considered in isolation but be studied as part of the country's political and economic history. The program ... was strongly dependent on the new Marxist view of literature, if not as narrow or dogmatic.[31]

Mailer later acknowledged that 'Harvard changed me profoundly',[32] for his education both there and in Paris with Jean Malaquais had prepared him for political activism. It was to the American left, and specifically to the anti-Cold War Progressive Citizens of America (PCA) that he gravitated in 1946. This group, which became the Progressive Party in 1948, was led by former Vice-President Henry Wallace. It is this politician who provides a crucial link with Mailer's first novel. Immediately after 1945 the American left was dividing between the PCA and the Americans for Democratic Action (ADA). Both groups criticised President Truman's foreign policy which they believed was responsible for inaugurating and perpetuating the Cold War. The PCA, however, was very much on the left, favouring a *rapprochement* with the Communists, while the ADA took a firm anti-Communist stance. Mailer joined the PCA and in 1948 became a party worker for the Wallace presidential campaign. According to his wife, Bea, also working for the Wallace bid, 'Norman and I wanted better relations with Russia, and we wanted to stop the Cold War. . . . Truman wasn't about to do it, and [Governor Thomas E.] Dewey would have been worse than Reagan. So Henry Wallace seemed like a viable alternative.'[33] Mailer visited Hollywood, making eighteen speeches for Wallace. According to Nigel Leigh, 'at least two years before the 1948 campaign, Mailer took seriously the Wallacite prediction that America was in danger of becoming fascist'.[34] It was this conviction which informed the political context of *The Naked and the Dead*.

Mailer's politics were to play an even more prominent role in his next novel, *Barbary Shore* (1951). With Malaquais as the *eminence gris* once more, he had begun to move away from Stalinism to embrace by 1949 a new revolutionary programme, summed up here by Norman Podhoretz:

> he soon lost faith in Marxism altogether. But here he diverged onto a track of his own. Whereas most ex-Trotskyist intellectuals of the thirties wound up in the fifties as enemies of the revolutionary idea altogether, Mailer in giving up on revolutionary socialism proclaimed himself the leader of a new revolution: a cultural rather than political revolution, a revolution that would 'move backward toward being and the secrets of human energy' instead of forward toward the struggle for control over a more and more highly industrialized world. In his own eyes, in other words, he was still a radical – indeed more of one than ever before.[35]

Barbary Shore is, however, a politically confused text. At various points in it Mailer can be seen to be broadly Marxist, Trotskyist, while 'towards the end it is strongly implied through symbols that he favours a post-Marxist radical position'.[36] According to Mailer, he 'finished the novel with a political position which was a far-flung mutation of Trotskyism'.[37] The grim surrealistic city of fear depicted in the novel is a reflection of Mailer's own artistic and political crisis at the start of the 1950s.

Soon after publication of *The Naked and the Dead* Mailer realised that, at the age of twenty-six, he had exhausted his existing store of life experience necessary for novel writing. In *Advertisements for Myself* (1959), in the 'Second Advertisement for Myself: Barbary Shore', he explains how his first novel had used up his biographical reservoir, saying:

> there was nothing left in the first twenty-four years of my life to write about; one way or another, my life seemed to have been mined and melted into the long reaches of the book. And so I was prominent and empty, and I had to begin life again.[38]

Years later he was to look back on *Barbary Shore* as 'the most imaginative of my novels',[39] though he has also said that 'what nobody has ever understood is that *Barbary Shore* is my most autobiographical novel'.[40] The novel is dedicated to Malaquais who influenced its futuristic *mise-en-scène*. This debt is also acknowledged in the 'Second Advertisement', but the novel's more important source lies beneath the surface, for as Mailer admitted, '*Barbary Shore* was really a book to emerge from the bombarded cellars of my unconscious.'[41] Mailer's exit from the cul-de-sac he faced after writing *The Naked and the Dead* was indeed 'to begin life again', though this regeneration would now be accomplished through the previously unexplored reaches of the psyche. The novel marks an important new departure then, and Mailer has always insisted on it as a key not only to the psychic climate of the 1950s, what he called 'the air of our time',[42] but also to his later work, which is also often alive to the unconscious sources of experience. *Barbary Shore* was a crisis in Mailer's development which he overcame, and in so doing he was party to the 'cultural cycle' of the 1950s, a generic feature of the decade in which, according to W. T. Lhamon, 'singly and collectively, people [in America] converted their crises to opportunities'.[43] In his own crisis of personal and artistic blockage, Mailer shared something with the broader mood of cultural flux in the United States. This was partly evident in 'the intense divisions troubling people at the time – the new cast of delinquency, the rights and suffrage struggles, the fears of communism and radioactive fallout'.[44] In the novel's vision of America's estate at this time, instability and anguish are at the centre. For Mailer *Barbary Shore* may be considered as 'the richest of my first three novels for it has in its high fevers a kind of insane insight into the psychic mysteries of Stalinists, secret policemen, narcissists, children, Lesbians, hysterics, revolutionaries'.[45] Perhaps the most enduring feature of *Barbary Shore* will be its evocation of mood, the mood of the American 1950s, manifest in the novel's plot of conspiracy and paranoia. As Norman Rosten put it, 'the book was a little confusing – you didn't quite know who or what anything was. But it had a magnetic, mysterious appeal at the time because in '51 everyone was screwed up that way'.[46]

While writing *Barbary Shore*, Mailer and Bea had moved to Hollywood. In so doing they were treading a path taken by previous American writers, most famously F. Scott Fitzgerald and William Faulkner. The year in Hollywood was later to contribute a good deal to Mailer's third novel, *The Deer Park* (1955), but while he was there the experience of writing film scripts proved no more fruitful and in some ways as damaging for him as for his literary predecessors. There was certainly a destructive effect on the Mailers' marriage, with one friend remembering Mailer's admission that Hollywood had 'corrupted' him – 'he was young, suddenly very famous, and he was wined and dined . . . people just fell over him. He also talked about this in the context of his break-up with Bea, how the time he was out there had been very bad for their marriage.'[47] Jean Malaquais, who with his wife had lived with the Mailers in Hollywood, also tells a similar story of marital discord caused by Mailer's new celebrity:

At first we lived in the house Norman and Bea had taken ear-

Introduction: The Shaping of Personality

lier in the Hollywood hills. Bea wasn't resentful at being in California, at least not at first. She was painting. She'd written a novel but couldn't get it published. Girls were flocking around Norman. He never confided in me about his activities, but I think he was quite responsive. Bea didn't have any friends of her own, though, and everything, of course, was centered on him. They quarrelled mightily . . . and they even fought physically.[48]

The Mailers had moved to Hollywood in 1949 after Samuel Goldwyn had offered the novelist a contract to write an original screenplay, which was to be based loosely on Nathanael West's novel of 1939, *Miss Lonelyhearts*. The picture of Mailer that emerges from Hilary Mills's biography is of a writer determined to avoid the artistic vitiation associated with American writers and Hollywood, a Mailer very different from the angry advocate of violent dissent who would emerge at the end of the 1950s. Bea Mailer remembers him as a self-divided figure in Hollywood, 'so afraid of instincts in himself that would make him what he actually later became that he checked them abnormally'.[49] Those instincts would later commit him to risk-taking as a positive necessity for human development, but while in Hollywood 'he was always turning down things'.[50] This was partly due to his desire to safeguard his political integrity, to avoid the compromises with his left-wing views which he thought would result from a closer relationship with the Hollywood ethos.

Although Mailer was 'one of the few literary celebrities in Hollywood who had no compunction about being identified with the left',[51] it is odd that he avoided the attentions of the House Un-American Activities Committee in its efforts to expose Communist subversion in the 1950s. But in Lillian Hellman's view, Mailer's Malaquais-inspired speech delivered at the Waldorf Peace Conference of 1949 'was undoubtedly the reason why he was never called before HUAC: he had announced to everybody that he was not a Stalinist and no longer had any sympathy with Communists. . . . He was a Trotskyist.'[52] Strangely, although he was never persecuted by HUAC, his father was, ostensibly because of his 'continuing close association [with a] concealed Communist',[53] namely his son. The charge was that Barney Mailer was what was known then as 'a loyalty risk' by virtue of this association. Mailer wrote an affidavit to the government's so-called 'Loyalty Board' on his father's behalf. This affidavit, which concluded with the following few lines of dialogue, had the desired consequence of convincing the American government that Barney Mailer was no Communist by association. The 'Mailers at Home' sketch mocked the ludicrous but very dangerous witch-hunting mentality which could put an ordinary American like Barney Mailer in the dock, suspected of guilt by 'close association':

> On those occasions when I continue my 'close association' with my parents, such as those evenings when I visit for dinner, the following conversation could probably be heard between my father and myself:
> *The Time*: (one of those rare times when politics is discussed.)
> *Norman Mailer*: I think the whole thing in Korea is hopeless. It's a pilot-light war. Ignorant Americans and ignorant Orientals are just butchering each other.
> *I. B. Mailer*: I don't know where an intelligent boy like you picks up such idiotic rubbish.
> *Fan Mailer* (the mother): Don't call him an idiot.
> *Norman Mailer*: Well, he's not so smart himself.
> *I. B. Mailer*: I never talked to my father the way you talk to me.

Mailer himself acknowledged later how empty his year in Hollywood was, saying 'I spent a year in Hollywood and I got less that I got from any two or three weeks in the army.'[55] This was probably due to his morally circumspect attitude at that time. Writing to a friend also about to spend some time as a writer in Hollywood, Mailer hands down some personal advice concerning the need to remain aware of its double standards:

> Enjoy Hollywood and keep your detachment. . . . But always bear in mind that people who work in Hollywood are like Stalinists . . . don't depend upon them when the chips are down,

Introduction: The Shaping of Personality

because their decisions can never be made on the basis of friendship alone. They have a public life more real than their private life.'[56]

Mailer's artistic response to Hollywood duplicity was to emerge over a year after his leaving there in June 1950, when he started work on *The Deer Park*, a novel with which he had great difficulty. Matters were in no sense helped by the break-up of his marriage in 1951. Fame and celebrity had proven too much for the marriage.

After the critical failure of *Barbary Shore* it was important this next novel restore some of Mailer's stature, but again the reviews were a sore disappointment to him. At the time Malcolm Cowley probably came closest to today's judgement of the novel, even though his review was one of the most favourable. He wrote that 'the book leaves us with the feeling that Norman Mailer, though not a finished novelist, is one of the two or three most talented writers of his generation'.[57] Brendan Gill in the *New Yorker* called *The Deer Park* the product of a 'reckless talent',[58] a judgement Mailer remembers with approval in *Advertisements for Myself*. A large part of the recklessness was certainly to be found in the novel's subject-matter, which concerns the depravity of the movie colony, Desert D'Or. Yet the novel also involves Mailer's desperate search for a new writing style, a style he could regard as his own. His first novel was clearly derivative, as he himself acknowledged; in its naturalism and social realism critics could easily discern the debts he owed to American novelists such as James Farrell, John Dos Passos, and Theodore Dreiser. In *Barbary Shore* the style is an uneasy mix, but in *The Deer Park* for the first time we catch a glimpse of what might be called the style of Mailer's 'middle period' – that which begins with *Advertisements for Myself* (1959) and concludes with his biography *Marilyn* (1973). He has referred to what he calls the novel's 'interim style', adding that 'I don't really feel that I had my own style until *Advertisements*.'[59]

In 'Fourth Advertisement for Myself: The Last Draft of *The Deer Park*', Mailer gives us what he calls 'the most accurate account I've ever written of myself'.[60] The 'account' is of a writer in crisis. At the time of publication it amounted to one of the most candid statements of its kind that had ever appeared, yet its very openness, its confession of angry and bruised egotism gave a new inflection to the old theme of the artist misunderstood. With *The Deer Park* having been rejected by seven New York publishers on grounds of obscenity, Mailer came to understand the extent to which American literary culture had degenerated into what he termed 'the cliques, fashions, vogues, snobs, snots, and fools, not to mention a dozen bureaucracies of criticism . . . the day was gone when people held on to your novels no matter what others might say'.[61] And so a sense of his being an outsider was born in him. The writer who, while in Hollywood, was observed to have still 'a kid's approach to the world' with 'something very sweet about him',[62] was on a darkening turn. The 'Fourth Advertisement' seems in retrospect to transcend the lone confessional of the autobiographer; in its realisation of radical disaffection from the times there sounds the first rumour of all that would break loose in the next decade in America, a decade of rebellion against the spiritual oppressions of middle-class conformity:

> I was out of fashion and that was the score . . . the publishing habits of the past were going to be of no help for my *Deer Park*. And so as the language of sentiment would have it, something broke in me, but I do not know if it was so much a loving heart, as a cyst on the weak, the unreal, and the needy, and I was finally open to my anger. I turned within my psyche I can almost believe, for I felt something shift to murder in me . . . I was an outlaw, a psychic outlaw, and I liked it, I liked it a good sight better than trying to be a gentleman, and with a set of emotions accelerating one on the other, I mined down deep into the murderous message of marijuana, the smoke of the assassins, and for the first time in my life I knew what it was to make your kicks.[63]

The novel was a major turning-point in Mailer's career. Both in its public reception and in its style and themes, it marks his farewell to what he called 'my adolescent crush on the profession

Introduction: The Shaping of Personality 15

of the writer',[64] and inaugurates, especially in its final pages, his first embrace of dissent as a necessary aspect of his philosophy of Hip. It sold around 50,000 copies, half of the number that would have satisfied Mailer. Paying him $10,000, the largest advance for a novel in his firm's century-long history, the president of Putnam's, Walter Minton, was not alone in believing that such relatively poor sales figures may well have affected Mailer's progress as a novelist, commenting that had '*The Deer Park* sold two or three times better, who knows, he might've been more inclined to go on with novels'.[65] As it was, Mailer was not to publish another novel for a decade, when he returned to the form with *An American Dream* in 1965. In *Advertisements* he referred to 'the devastations of creative reserve which the forced last draft of *The Deer Park* had burned across my brain',[66] another version of the crisis he had faced after the publication of *The Naked and the Dead*. If that novel had all but exhausted the creative potential of his own life experience, he now feared that the very spring of creativity was running dry. When the personally inscribed copy of *The Deer Park* which he had sent to Ernest Hemingway was returned with the package unopened, stamped 'Return to Sender', his self-esteem took a final plunge. Although in later years Hemingway said he had never received a copy of the novel, according to Hilary Mills he 'must have bought a copy himself . . . for in December 1955 he wrote to his friend Wallace Meyer, "in *The Deer Park*, Mailer really blows the whistle on himself"'.[67] Turned down by seven publishers, and now perhaps ignored or damned by his literary exemplar, Mailer was moving into a period of personal, aesthetic, and philosophical revision, into what he called 'unbalanced heroics'. 'I was on the edge of many things and I had more than a bit of violence in me.'[68]

The violence in Mailer was to issue forth at numerous points in years to come, having its most famous literary apologia in his essay of 1957 'The White Negro', and on a personal level reaching its infamous nadir in his stabbing of his then wife, Adele, in 1960. Mailer had married Adele Morales in 1954. Adele, a Peruvian, was a painter and living in Greenwich Village, the New York bohemian neighbourhood to which Mailer moved in the winter of 1951 after the separation from Bea. Shortly before beginning her relationship with Mailer, Adele had been involved with Jack Kerouac, and was very much a part of the Greenwich Village scene at the time. Hilary Mills offers this assessment of the way Adele's personality and temperament both shaped and changed Mailer:

> Adele would be the radical change Mailer was looking for . . . and for the next tempestuous decade the couple would be inseparable. Beatrice had been in many ways like Mailer's mother – strong, bright, Jewish, and intolerant of Norman's macho antics. But Adele was quite different: a dark, sensuous Latin, who, at least initially, was a strong woman without a sense of her own strength. . . . Yet as an artist Adele had her own unconventional imagination and she would learn to play Mailer's psychic games with innovation. . . . Although these games would eventually get out of hand as Mailer's vision of the 'orgiastic and violent' intensified, in the beginning Adele offered Mailer an exciting and mysterious departure from the dominant women he had known. . . . Adele's responsive sensuality stimulated Mailer's evolving sense of freedom and his growing desire for the forbidden.[69]

The years that followed the break with Beatrice were to be convulsive ones in Mailer's life, enfolding what Mills calls 'his spiritual trial: years dominated by sensuality, drugs, confusion, disturbing insights into his own violence'.[70]

Mailer's bitter and growing sense of alienation from American mores was, throughout the Eisenhower years of the 1950s, to express itself in an increasingly revolutionary ideology until, in 'First Advertisement for Myself', he could say, without irony, 'the sour truth is that I am imprisoned with a perception which will settle for nothing less than making a revolution in the consciousness of our time'. The 'revolution' was to involve him in a mighty assault upon the American psyche. Mailer's presence on the American scene was, it sometimes seemed, ubiquitous. It was as though having once felt the pain of exclusion from the mainstream after the failure of *The Deer Park*, he was determined to involve himself so thoroughly in both mainstream and tributar-

Introduction: The Shaping of Personality

ies that throughout the 1950s and especially the 1960s his voice and America's were one and the same. 'So goes Mailer, so goes America' as Wilfrid Sheed once said, and no one has expressed Mailer's involvement with American reality better than Alfred Kazin:

> what was creative in this 'role' was Mailer's belief in the validity of his most private thoughts. He made his fantasies interesting to many Americans . . . the Mailer who became such a laughable, publicizable part of the American consciousness was always there because he had somehow turned his most private wishes and fears into public symbols. Mailer accomplished what few novelists were still able to do – he made his mind public. He was definitely not one of that minority group which will always feel excluded from the great American reality. He was inside this reality and on every side of it . . . the voraciousness of American life, its power in human affairs, its fury of transformation had found in Mailer a writer who would always find any and all of it 'credible'.[71]

Mailer's ideology was developing from a blend of politics, mysticism and existentialism: as the decade of the 1950s progressed he began to refine further his attack upon modern society, and to target in detail what he called the totalitarianism of American culture. Totalitarianism in his demonology is a many-headed monster, though as Christopher Brookeman notes, 'Mailer uses the term totalitarian to describe a process of dehumanisation that was as evident in the culture of American capitalism as in that of Soviet Russia.'[72] After *The Deer Park*, Mailer's work in both fiction and non-fiction is, at least for a decade and a half, almost wholly concerned with what he regarded as the malignant effects of totalitarianism in American society. As the next decade progressed with the war in Vietnam, the increasing hostilities between left and right in America, and the ever more obvious evidence of the violence meted out by the state to ensure conformity to its politics and norms, his analysis came to be regarded as historically acute. What Kazin would call

Mailer's 'psychic intuition into . . . the experience of our time'[73] began to express itself.

Mailer himself explains what he calls 'the phenomenon of Norman Mailer' as obtaining its vatic capacity from his use of drugs, particularly marijuana, commencing in the mid-1950s. He told an interviewer that it was in 1955 'when I started smoking pot and seeing myself from the inside and the outside both. The inside and the outside: I could go back and forth every five or ten seconds in my head.'[74] There can be little doubt that his use and advocation of drugs contributed to his being accepted as one of the most influential voices in the left-liberal counterculture of the 1960s. Similarly, his emergence as an exponent of a theory of sexuality which saw the sexual act as existentially liberating and also linked sexuality with creativity was a further validation of Mailer's status as a radical ideologue. The Mailer who begins to emerge in the mid-1950s is indeed a 'phenomenon', if by that term one refers to his energetic self-promotions, all of them either directly or indirectly aspects of a new revolutionary sensibility. Norman Podhoretz remembers the extent to which Mailer's presence and ideas served as a standard of radical hope for those, like himself, feeling political despair in the wake of their rejection of Marxism. For those on the beleaguered left of American politics, Mailer represented an example for the radical imagination to follow:

> Bored with my own sensibly moderate liberal ideas, but with Marxism and all its variants closed off as an alternative, I saw in Mailer the possibility of a new kind of radicalism. . . . Soon there would be others, but at that moment there was no one else in sight who held out the same tantalizing possibility . . . he was bold and he was daring; and he wanted to be great.[75]

By far the most important articulation of Mailer's radicalism was his essay of 1957, 'The White Negro', but before its publication, Mailer had helped to found the *Village Voice*, a newspaper addressing itself to the bohemian community of Greenwich Village. The first issue of the newspaper came out in 1955, coinciding with the publication of *The Deer Park*. Mailer's brief tenure as one of the newspaper's editors is biographically significant in several ways. Firstly, his regular contributions as a columnist show clearly the new direction of his thought at the time. As co-editor Jerry Tallmer remembers, Mailer had very definite ideas about the paper's political orientations – 'Norman's idea, I think, was for the paper to be a hip shock sheet . . . he wanted the *Voice* to deal in a *Daily News* way with the new subjects of drugs, jazz, the swinging black scene, and sexuality, all under the aegis of "anti-Establishment"'.[76] These objectives were not ones shared by Mailer's co-editors and led in April 1956 to his departure from the staff. In the 'Fifth Advertisement for Myself', he explains his strategy and targets while with the *Village Voice*: referring to himself as 'general Marijuana', his new *nom de guerre*, Mailer explicitly links the new militancy of his views with his reaction to *The Deer Park*'s failure. The novelist would become the radical *provocateur*; the 'Advertisement' here, written in 1958, clearly shows Mailer's remarkable intuition into the gathering strength of dissident values. The piece is also a striking example of his new stridency of attitude – unabashedly casting himself in the role of revolutionary warrior-hero:

> There were odds that it would take months, or even years to get back what I had given to the book [*The Deer Park*] . . . it was not the season then to pick up again on the private habits of a novel. At heart, I wanted a war, and the Village was already glimpsed as the field for battle . . . I had the feeling of an underground revolution on its way, and I do not know that I was wrong . . . I was ready too early but I still wonder if the kind of newspaper I wanted might not have managed to give a little speed to that moral and sexual revolution which is yet to come upon us . . . the column began as the declaration of my private war on American journalism, mass communications, and the totalitarianism of totally pleasant personality.[77]

Mailer's brief tenure as an editor of and contributor to the *Village Voice* would be the forcing-ground for much that would sustain him throughout the coming decade. The writing he did for the newspaper was, as he said, 'the first lick of fire in a new American consciousness', and signalled his epic ambition to be 'a hero of my time'.[78]

Mailer's personal life was to a large degree reflecting the public statements of the self-styled 'psychic outlaw'. With a vision of sex as 'the sword of history', he was 'drawing upon hash, lush, Harlem, Spanish wife, Marxist culture',[79] and generally forcing himself into states of mind and experience for which his views in 'The White Negro' would partly be apologia. Social outrage and non-conformity in his own relations with others were to become an integral part of the hipster's disposition. In Mailer's second marriage, violence, or the temptation to risk violence, was becoming an aspect of the relationship. Walter Minton, a friend of the Mailers, remembers one instance of this:

> I don't know whether Norman pushed at Adele the way he later did with Beverley, but . . . in '58 or thereabouts we had a party . . . for a lot of publishing people, and afterwards Peter [Israel] and his then wife Nancy didn't have a ride back to the city, so they went with Norman. Norman got caught behind a slow-moving car in the Lincoln Tunnel, and Adele told him to pass anyway, yelling, 'You're chicken, you're scared. You're always telling me not to be afraid. Now you're scared!' So Norman goes out and around. *Zoom!* I guess the on-coming truck gave way or something. Peter said he was petrified. She was goading him and I've always thought of that story when I think of what happened a few years later. [a reference to Mailer's stabbing Adele in 1960] I can almost see her – I swear to God – whatever happened, whatever brought that on, saying, 'You haven't got the guts'.[80]

Irving Howe, the editor of the journal *Dissent*, which published 'The White Negro' in 1957, has recognised the extent to which the essay was 'an endorsement of violence'.[81] Mailer's code hero, the hipster, is a 'philosophical psychopath' who understands that the violence of the totalitarian system – dehumanising and threatening to extinguish individualism – at times requires a violent response. Certainly, as Chandler Brossard comments, the violence was not confined to Mailer's ideology, for his relationship with Adele 'would grow progressively more violent over the next four years'.[82] Those close to the Mailers at the time have referred to their 'very deep-seated violent relationship'[83] and to the sense of continual tension in the marriage. Mailer's increasing aggression also found an outlet in his taking up boxing, the beginning of his lifelong interest in the sport. Unfortunately, he could not confine himself to the ring or the punchbags he had installed in his studio, and would quite often pick fights with any who seemed to him fair game. He was, according to one of his best friends, 'making a fetish out of being rude'.[84]

With 'The White Negro', Mailer would establish himself as a prophet of the times, showing that he was 'earlier than anybody to pick up advance notes on what was coming – he clearly foresaw the sixties'.[85] The essay was a landmark on the road to that 'moral and sexual revolution' he had looked forward to while with the *Village Voice*, a culture-reading which would have enormous impact on the age:

> The strands of theory and experience that Mailer strung together in the essay would help form the basis of the new counter-culture which emerged in the late 1960s. Fighting his own lonely battle against the establishment, Mailer had presaged the mass adoption of marijuana, youth rebellion, mysticism, the black revolution, violent confrontation, existentialism, anti-totalitarianism, anti-militarism, all of it enveloped in a pastiche of Freud and Marx, a mix that was to become the new religion of the upcoming generation.[86]

The essay was also Mailer's amendment to the philosophy of the so-called Beat Generation, epitomised by the writing of Jack Kerouac and Allen Ginsberg. Kerouac, who met Mailer in 1958, had, most famously in his novel *On the Road*, voiced the mood of American youth in the mid-1950s, and reacted negatively to Mailer's more abrasive and confrontational adaptation of Beat philosophy. Ginsberg remembers that a part of his own and Kerouac's response was due to their feeling that Mailer's version of the Beat rebel was a fundamental distortion of what for them had been its essence. As Ginsberg remarked, the whole point of *On the Road* ... as well as all of [William] Burroughs' writing, all of mine, and everything else going on with the Beat thing had to do with American tender-heartedness. ... Norman's notion of the hipster as being cool and psychopathic ... was a kind of macho folly that we giggled at.[87]

Yet despite such reservations Ginsberg was also able to see just how significant 'The White Negro' was. A good deal of the essay's importance was due to its having been written by Norman Mailer. The cultural status of the novelist as artist was still a very exalted one in the 1950s. As Jules Feiffer put it,

> in the fifties and even early sixties novelists were thought of as very important people. This died out in the seventies, but back then one still thought of Hemingway and Fitzgerald and Sinclair Lewis as having incredible stature, and Mailer was one of two or three Americans clearly destined to follow in their footsteps.[88]

For Ginsberg, Mailer was, then, a potent recruit; to find in him a philosophical ally meant that the moral and sexual revolution – until then a reality only in the world of Beat bohemia and underground – was suddenly being promoted by one of the most important young writers of the day. As Ginsberg remembered, 'it was the most intelligent statement I'd seen by any literary-critical person, anyone acquainted with the great world of literature ... I saw him as a knight in armour charging to the rescue'.[89] And so with 'The White Negro' Mailer became 'the outlaw' of the literary Establishment while at the same time, as Ginsberg understood, lending some of his mainstream legitimacy to the ideology of the outlaw as set out in the essay. His willingness to absorb the Beat mentality, and to modify it in his own way, were early signs of his empathy with American subcultures, something that set Mailer apart from his contemporaries who were, as Hilary Mills notes, 'aware that Mailer's work was moving in a radically different direction from that of most of the post-World War II writers'.[90]

'The White Negro' would become the most famous piece in *Advertisements for Myself*, which Mailer published two years later in 1959. Ernest Hemingway described *Advertisements* as that 'ragtag assembly of his rewrites, second thoughts and ramblings shot through with occasional brilliance'[91] and the book is best seen as one of Mailer's most definitive stylesheets, combining ideology with autobiography, and more than any other of his books proclaiming his new identity. 'I was trying to end a certain part of my literary life and begin anew', he has said. With *Advertisements*, 'I wanted to declare myself, put myself on stage firmly and forever.'[92] The new book accomplished this aim, boldly declaring its author's secession from the narrow enclave of traditional literary endeavour. Having with the tally of his first three novels scored 'victory, disaster, and draw', Mailer would now leave the restrictions and disappointments of that arena for a decade, perhaps sensing the emergence of a new, wider audience in a mass America of proliferating subcultures. William Phillips, co-editor of *Partisan Review*, regarded Mailer as one of the first beneficiaries of this process:

> The prejudice against Mailer on the part of some people that he was lowbrow or middlebrow because he'd had a huge popular success was gradually being wiped out, partly by the obvious intellectual concerns in *Advertisements for Myself* and partly because the whole question of middlebrow and highbrow was beginning to evaporate. The atmosphere was beginning to change, with the popular media opening up to the more serious figures . . . and certainly the development of paperbacks was also narrowing the gap. Norman was thus a true crossover figure, publishing in *Partisan Review* and *Playboy* both, and I can't think of anybody who did it quite the same way.[94]

Yet the irony was that it was *Advertisements* that got Mailer the seal of Establishment approval. He was critically blessed by Diana and Lionel Trilling who, between them, had at the time enormous power in New York literary culture. He was taken up by them and by the New York intelligentsia of which they were king and queen, and became their 'crazy and sometimes dangerous' genius. Irving Howe remembers Mailer's impact, 'I always thought he was incredibly smart, and so did Trilling too. And Diana even more so . . . he was our genius, "our" meaning the New York intellectual group.'[95]

Just as Mailer had seen the cultural importance and appeal of the Beat movement and had given its themes his own revision in 'The White Negro', so the New York critics also seeing the inevitability of such changes, elected Mailer, not Ginsberg or Kerouac, their spokesman. This was partly due to background affinities – Mailer, the middle-class Jew educated at Harvard, had never quite overcome the standards of social deference and respect for authority deriving from his background. For him, the Trillings represented what Diana Trilling called 'conscience figures of the time'.[96] Good manners and a good suit were always available as essential features of that protocol of respect Mailer acknowledged. 'With people like me and Trilling', says Howe,

> he kept the skills to present his Howe face, his Trilling face. The day before seeing either of us he might have been on a terrible drunk, and he might repeat it the day after, but when he came to us he was able to show himself just as he wanted to – suit, tie, vest, the whole stylized deal straight from Oxford.[97]

By all accounts the Trillings liked Mailer and were 'sort of fascinated by his "wickedness"'.[98] Compared to Ginsberg and Burroughs, Mailer must have seemed to offer an instance of the devil known. But also his revision of beatnik into hipster in 'The White Negro' was ultimately a conservative assimilation of the phenomenon; a substantial part of the appeal *Advertisements* had for the Trillings and their circle was due to its being a powerful model of both literary analysis and cultural criticism. Mailer in *Advertisements* revealed his aptitude for the kind of cultural critique depending upon rational, analytically probing thought which had not often been regarded as the province of the novelist. In doing so, he was able to show his right to sit at the same table as the likes of Trilling and Howe, whose cultural status derived from the authority vested in them as literary critics and

Introduction: The Shaping of Personality 25

cultural commentators. The revelation of his talent in this direction was one very important 'self' Mailer was advertising in the book. So a concealed irony of 'The White Negro', perhaps not missed by those in the New York intelligentsia who took him up, is that in proposing, arguing for and analysing the cultural conditions giving rise to the hipster, Mailer was *ipso facto* demonstrating his own shortcomings as an exemplar of the species. Certainly the essay showed his remoteness from the Beats themselves, who were never interested in analysing their activity, just in doing it. So much was noticed by Mailer's most enthusiastic champion, Norman Podhoretz, who published a ground-breaking essay on him in *Partisan Review* in 1957, and saw quite clearly the intellectual in Mailer as the mark of distinction in the comparison:

> I thought that Ginsberg, Kerouac, and the Beats were discrediting the whole radical impulse . . . I was looking for a certain combination of qualities, and for me Mailer had it. . . . Unlike the Beats, *he brought mind and discipline* to bear on the eruption of instinct . . . if there was to be a revolution in consciousness, Mailer's was the way to make it.[99] (my emphasis)

Mailer, with *Advertisements*, had found that in challenging the Establishment, by collecting examples of his writings – good, bad or mediocre – and subjecting them to the kind of critical scrutiny he believed they had failed to receive from the critics, he was suddenly and ironically hailed as the Establishment's model of the cultural revolutionary, the acceptable face of the radical.

It often seems that Mailer's wild years (which he himself dates as 1954–60 – 'I burned out my brain in those years'[100]) involved experimenting with extreme, often violent states of mind; there is a strong sense of the programmatic about it all, as though the life was lived partly as a means of self-consciously effecting that character transformation he had referred to in the 'Fifth Advertisement'. 'I was anxious above all else to change a hundred self-defeating habits',[101] he wrote there, and the picture that emerges from a diversity of first-hand accounts is of a writer exploring the 'shift to murder' in his psyche partly at least in order to write about it. Mailer's subject after his first three novels – none of which was written in the first person – was Mailer himself, though of course a Mailer portrayed as having had experiences which validate his credentials as spokesman for many. In order to make those credentials fit the new role of 'psychic outlaw' he self-consciously created the conditions necessary to that role. The 'burned-out brain' was an essential part of the mythology, though Mailer wrapped large parts of the brain in fireproof material – the writer always having priority over the violent debauchee:

> I used to see him at parties and it would bother me. Toward the end of the evening he'd often become aggressive and unpleasant. . . he didn't want to be conventional or square. He was afraid, maybe, of ageing, but I felt he was making a mistake the way he did it – all the idiocy of running around with those violent people, being almost out of control. The amazing thing is that he protected his time to work. Party hour wouldn't start until later. He'd never get up in the morning and start drinking.[102]

Yet the Mailer who was seen as 'an animal, a bully'[103] in Provincetown society where he and Adele had been summering in the late 1950s, could also be remembered by historian Arthur Schlesinger, Jr as 'a man of distinguished manners'[104] throughout the twenty years of their acquaintance. The picture that emerges from Peter Manso's collage of witnesses is of Mailer the white negro, and Mailer the still-dedicated writer; put too sharply together and the images conflate into a life of careerist enterprise based upon narcissism, amorality and the calculated flouting of social norms, a personality perfectly aware of the cultural value of shock, particularly to those like the New York group, so influential in making or breaking writers' reputations. Irving Howe acknowledges that 'while Mailer was crazy and sometimes dangerous – which I still believe – he was still able to get at certain things we could not. We admired it, I think even envied it.'[105] Mailer was indeed 'crazy and sometimes dangerous', as the stabbing of Adele was soon to prove, yet he took care

Introduction: The Shaping of Personality

never to bring that instability too close to those, like Howe or Trilling, who were prepared to tolerate it as the price to be paid for unusual insights. 'Culture is worth a little risk' was one of Mailer's most publicised remarks, and in the years being discussed, he took considerable risks not only with his own sanity but with the lives of those in his company.

Given the urge to violence in Mailer's relations with others, it did not come as a surprise to some that his marriage reached a bloody culmination. The facts are that in the early hours of 20 November 1960, Mailer had given a party to celebrate and publicise his candidacy for the mayoralty of New York city; by the end of the party, in a state of drunken meanness, he took a knife and stabbed Adele in the abdomen and back. She was taken to New York University Hospital in a critical condition, and required extensive surgery. Mailer was arrested by the police and as a result of a medical report which found that he was 'having an acute paranoid breakdown with delusional thinking and is both homicidal and suicidal',[106] admitted to Bellevue mental hospital for further observation. The magistrate who ordered Mailer's committal told him 'your recent history indicates that you cannot distinguish fiction from reality',[107] while Mailer insisted on his sanity. He was in Bellevue for just two weeks before being discharged as legally sane. Adele subsequently refused to press criminal charges against her husband, and refused to sign a complaint. Though the presiding magistrate of the Felony Court believed that 'a probable crime' had been committed and sent the case to the higher Grand Jury Court of New York County, it was there, almost a year later, that Mailer received a suspended sentence with a probation period not to exceed three years. The Mailers' marriage was to be formally dissolved two years later.

There can be no doubt that for those who know little about Mailer's life and work, the stabbing is part of the little they know. Mailer himself has said 'a decade's anger made me do it. After that, I felt better.'[108] Hilary Mills concludes her chapter titled 'The Stabbing' by linking the work and the life, suggesting that 'in stabbing Adele he had acted out the ultimate psychopathy he had expressed in 'The White Negro'.[109] Certainly his friends and those who had been present at the party on the night of the stabbing differ in their responses to and interpretations of Mailer's behaviour. Some see him as a victim of the times, rather than casting him in the role of protagonist as does Mills. So H. L. Humes, a co-founder of the *Paris Review* and at the time of the incident a neighbour and friend of the Mailers, is more than willing to explain the stabbing as an expression of cultural dysfunction:

> The whole period was so bizarre I can't even begin to describe it. . . . But the hiatus between Kennedy's election and his inauguration was the period when the hammer came down. The stabbing seemed like a turning-point, and people became genuinely terrified . . . some people tried to dismiss it, some tried to explain it away as just Norman's craziness. But even his enemies realized that he wasn't functioning at his normal level, and, indeed, a fair number of people saw what was ailing him as ailing themselves. But I look upon the years of '59 to '62, with the Bay of Pigs, as some kind of watershed of evil. You can't underestimate this. Even the weather was weird – an Indian summer with clammy days. It was almost as if somebody had been out to totally overturn the applecart before Kennedy ever put foot in the White House, and here was one of America's finest writers literally cracking up in front of our eyes.[110]

A violent act to begin one of America's most violent decades, with Mailer a bellweather of all that was adrift. The nation was on the cusp of the most tragic self-examination since its Civil War exactly 100 years previously, lurching from the neurotic conformities of the 1950s into a decade of assassinations, race riots and political confrontations, all of this domestic fury being inflamed by the war in Vietnam. It was the decade that would see Mailer flourish in its angers; in his life and his work, in the novels *An American Dream* (1965), and *Why Are We in Vietnam?* (1967), and in works of creative journalism like *Miami and the Siege of Chicago* (1968) and especially *The Armies of the Night* (1968), his voice would address the pathology of an America at war with itself.

Introduction: The Shaping of Personality 29

Against this grim retrospect, his own most personal blood-letting seems to find its apologia; for many who knew him, his was but a more extreme case:

> When I went back to the city from the Cape it was a mad time, a freeing for myself in a way but also quite hysterical. We were all sort of square, middle-class, hardworking kids from hardworking environments . . . then suddenly, *whoosh*, it didn't work. The pressures were building, and we all exploded, each in our own way. Norman went farther out, but then again, Norman was the role model.[111]

Others were at least willing to suggest the part played by Adele in the act, bringing it on herself – not a victim, but a reckless goader provoking Mailer to stab her – 'she started talking about his masculinity, making fun of him, and that's the one thing Norman can never take, someone denigrating his sexual vigor'.[112] Another friend, Eileen Finletter, admits she 'didn't have much sympathy for Adele, because I didn't like her . . . I thought she was like one of Saul Bellow's wives, absolute hell . . . instinctively I felt it was her fault, even though I knew Norman had probably been drinking, taking drugs, doing the whole bit'.[113] For Fanny Mailer the case against Adele was even more decisive – 'he stabbed Adele because of anger. She drove him to it, and she could drive anybody nuts.'[114]

For many it seems that Mailer's violence was tolerated as an inevitable aspect of his 'crazy genius', and the stabbing was understood in such a forgiving context. Mailer himself was anxious to prove he was not crazy at the time, since despite his defence of the psychopath in 'The White Negro', if he were committed to a psychiatric hospital for detention all his subsequent writing, he argued, 'would be considered that of a disordered mind'.[115] So, many regard Mailer as a victim – of the times, of a personality disorder which, somehow, he was not responsible for. Irving Howe, speaking for the New York critics, contributes to the consensus:

> People felt it was a tragedy, that a man had been driven to do

something that he didn't really want or intend to do, that he'd lost control. Among the 'uptown intellectuals' there was this feeling of shock and dismay, and I don't remember anyone judging him. The feeling was that he'd been driven to this by compulsiveness, by madness. He was seen as a victim. Nobody I knew thought that Norman was simply or coldly acting out some idea.[116]

Lionel Trilling, however, 'insisted that it wasn't a clinical situation but a conscious bad act . . . Norman was testing the limits of evil in himself'.[117] Both Mailer and the psychiatrist at Bellevue insisted on his sanity. If sane, then the following account of Mailer's psychological condition, by friend and fellow-novelist Chandler Brossard, is acute. Seeing him as one without 'a fundamental sensibility', Brossard argues that 'the scary thing' about Mailer was that 'he was willing to become a victim of ecstasy. He was capable of the ultimate act for his own purposes, without thinking of the effects on other people'.[118] Adele, the real victim of the stabbing, is still traumatised by its memory:

> It was when we moved that Norman began to develop those mannerisms, the accents, which he had never used before with me. He became a different person. Something was happening that was very, very, very wrong. . . . But I can't talk about the thing, what happened. It's too painful. And it did . . . well, it changed my life. I've had to learn to let go of the past and concentrate on today. There are certain things, no matter how much therapy, that are painful, that even with a therapist arouse too much when you dredge them up. I can't go into it. It stirs up too much, that's all.[119]

In contrast with Adele's trauma, the stabbing did no wound to Mailer's ascendancy as a celebrity. As Hilary Mills remarks,

> Mailer had in some way been victorious. He had thrust himself into public consciousness more swiftly and completely with this one nightmarish act than he could have done with perhaps a decade of serious, sustained work.[120]

Introduction: The Shaping of Personality

It can even be argued that his work from 'The White Negro' to *The Armies of the Night* is given added credibility as a result of the act; no longer a mere bystander, Mailer had become a participant in the national swing to violence at home and abroad. The next ten years would confirm the predictive nature of central themes of his work in the 1950s, as violence, war, non-conformity and the exploration of the individual's relationship with the state and its systems became issues which burst and boil on the surface of the American experience. For the young in America at that time, it was Mailer to whom they listened. He was:

> alone among living American writers, potentially Gargantuan. He could fight, speak, act and marry with a kind of overwhelming dexterity that sent waves of excitement into our imagination. That he had stabbed his wife (and got away with it) and been observed at Bellevue actually enhanced the image.... We looked for an intellectual hero who transcended, even flouted, the respectability of intellectualism.... We suspected Mailer could become the hero of our generation.[121]

But if the young looked to Mailer as a hero fit for the times, Mailer was in the process of doing some hero-building himself. One of his finest essays on American politics, 'Superman Comes to the Supermarket', derives from his meeting with John F. Kennedy in the summer of 1960 and his attendance at the Democratic Party Convention in Los Angeles in July of that year. In terms of its themes, its style and its impact, this essay – published in *Esquire* magazine in October 1960 and subsequently included in *The Presidential Papers* three years later – ranks as one of the author's most important contributions to American literature in the 1960s. According to Christopher Brookeman, the essay was an attempt to 'transform the nature of political journalism' and played a major part in 'making documentary political journalism a major genre in post-war America'.[122] Mailer was to argue in later years that the essay played a significant role in securing Kennedy's election to the presidency in January 1961. Clay Felker, editor of *Esquire* in 1960, believes the claim is not without foundation. Kennedy, says Felker, 'articulated an appeal to young Americans. Just as those of us who were the editors were reflecting that change – we were not Eisenhower-age people, we were a new generation – here was a new political figure for whom Mailer more than made the case.'[123] Considering Kennedy's posthumous exaltation as martyred hero, Mailer's piece with its stress on Kennedy's potentiality as a leader of vision and courage is an extraordinary adumbration of subsequent events. In terms of his later work, the 'Superman' essay was his first effort at a genre (later dubbed 'the New Journalism') in which he would excel. More than any other writer of the day, he brought to the politics of America in the 1960s a transfiguring profundity, an ability to see, with quick double vision, both the surfaces of American politics and its personalities as well as a willingness to sound the depths.

Mailer and Adele met the Kennedys at Hyannisport, the Kennedy summer residence, in August 1960. The young presidential candidate (Kennedy had won the Democratic nomination over Adlai Stevenson earlier that year) – who would always show he had media-savvy – was, as Felker remembers, in the months of his presidential campaign, 'very aware of the power of magazines'.[124] Kennedy and his staff were aware that Mailer was about to write 'a very important piece'[125] for *Esquire* magazine which at that time had great impact on opinion leaders. They were, though, apprehensive about Mailer's unpredictability and the meeting began with Kennedy making a calculatedly flattering reference to *The Deer Park*. Considering his sensitivity on the subject of his novels and their reputation, the remark had ingratiating results. As Mailer remembers:

> What struck me most about the interview was a passing remark whose importance was invisible on the scale of politics, but was altogether meaningful to my particular competence. As we sat down for the first time, Kennedy smiled nicely and said that he had read my books. One muttered one's pleasure. 'Yes,' he said, 'I've read . . . ' and then there was a short pause . . . 'I've read *The Deer Park* and . . . the others,' which startled me for it was the first time in a hundred similar situations, talking to someone whose knowledge of my work was

Introduction: The Shaping of Personality 33

casual, that the sentence did not come out, 'I've read *The Naked and the Dead* and the others'.[126]

Mailer divorced his second wife in 1962, and in the same year he married Lady Jeanne Campbell, daughter of the Duke of Argyll and granddaughter of Lord Beaverbrook. The marriage, which was, according to Mailer, 'a kind of bloodless hell, the sort I deserved, I fear, as a first payment on my sins',[127] lasted only a year, and though the match seemed improbable in many ways, Hilary Mills sees Lady Jeanne as a perfect complement to Mailer at that time, with the climb out of social disgrace after the stabbing of Adele as not the least of the new opportunities offered by the marriage. 'Many saw his marriage to Lady Jeanne Campbell as a search for respectability after his notoriety with Adele . . . she also guaranteed the writer increased visibility in the media.' For the Jewish boy from Brooklyn, she was, according to his first wife, Bea, 'the ultimate *shiksa*',[128] and the next step up the gentile social ladder.

At the very top was the Camelot of the Kennedys, and Mailer turned his attention to its queen in his essay 'An Evening with Jackie Kennedy', published in 1962. The piece raised a storm on publication, for in it Mailer, who had been refused an interview by the First Lady, took the opportunity to lecture her on her public responsibilities as 'queen of the arts' and America's Muse. He focused on the televised 'tour of the White House' given by Jackie Kennedy in 1962. From her manufactured voice ('one had heard better ones at Christmastime in Macy's selling gadgets to the grim'), to her delivery ('she had that intense wooden lack of rest, that lack of comprehension for each word offered up which one finds only in a few of those curious movie stars who are huge box office'), the portrait is one stressing her awful phoniness.[129] She had failed her potentialities as a saving symbol for an America which, in Mailer's view, cried out for inspiring leadership. Instead of presenting a strong sense of self, the self on display in 'An Evening with Jackie Kennedy' contributed to Mailer's developing analysis of national dysfunction. His culture-reading here is important, not least because it pre-dates Kennedy's assassination a year later, so modifying the view that the assassination was the sudden, first rip in the national consciousness. The inauthenticity of the First Lady was another sign that for Mailer, America in 1962 was already 'a nation which is not well':[130]

> Afterward one could ask what it was one wanted of her, and the answer was that she show herself to us as she is. Because what we suffer from in America, in that rootless moral wilderness of our expanding life, is the unadmitted terror in each of us that bit by bit, year by year, we are going mad. . . . Because our tragedy is that we diverge as countrymen further and further away from one another, like a space ship broken apart in flight which now drifts mournfully in isolated orbits, satellites to each other, planets none, communication faint.[131]

When Mailer completed his second miscellany *The Presidential Papers* in 1963, readers found the piece on Jackie Kennedy republished under the title 'The Existential Heroine', a companion piece now beside the 'Superman' essay on J.F.K., newly titled 'The Existential Hero'. The book as a whole proposed a new politics, what Mailer called 'existential politics'. Rooted in 'the concept of the hero, it would argue that the hero is the one kind of man who *never* develops by accident, that a hero is a consecutive set of brave and witty self-creations'.[132] America desperately needed a regeneration out of the flatness of the 1950s, and Mailer's thesis in these essays is that this can only be accomplished by a rediscovered ethic of bold personality. Public figures should become symbols for the unification of mass sensibility, a corrective to that cultural fragmentation described above. Presidents, First Ladies, sporting heroes, and, of course, writers like Norman Mailer (who had set out to match up to his own 'consecutive set of brave and witty self-creations') were all capable of stirring 'the telepathic logic of the unconscious'[133] in America at large. In *The Presidential Papers* Mailer's voice emerged as a carefully structured combination of the irreverent and the mystic.

As the decade progressed, Mailer's willingness to propose and to take up political radicalism began to characterise his public profile. The decade as a whole would eventually become his most prolific, with novels (*An American Dream* and *Why Are We in Vietnam?*), essay collections (*The Presidential Papers* and *Cannibals and Christians*), and works of creative journalism (*The Armies of the Night, Miami and the Siege of Chicago* and *Of a Fire on the Moon*) establishing his reputation as America's most important writer. The collective achievement remains an extraordinary record of his energies in full flood. Mailer had not only found his time, he had also helped to create it. On 2 May 1965, he spoke at the so-called Vietnam Day rally at the Berkeley campus of the University of California, and made a speech that became a key moment in the emergence of countercultural rebellion. According to both Jerry Rubin and Abbie Hoffman, the speech gave a provocative new dimension to the anti-Vietnam movement. Mailer exhorted his mainly young audience to advertise their opposition to American destruction in Vietnam by the symbolical expedient of taking a photograph of President Lyndon Johnson and displaying it upside down. Jerry Rubin remembers that 'when Norman got up and gave his speech – an extraordinary speech – the crowd went crazy. It was the first time anybody had made fun of the President.'[134] For Edward De Grazia, who organised the Legal Defense Committee of the Mobilization Against the War in Vietnam, Mailer's Berkeley speech is remembered as one of the first to say 'we've got to stop the war and somehow act. It seemed to be one of the first calls to action.'[135]

The speech was eventually published in the collection *Cannibals and Christians* (1966), a gathering of Mailer's writings since 1960. With more than a touch of irony, he dedicated the volume to Lyndon Johnson, 'whose name inspired young men to cheer for me in public'. The essays are of a literary, political, philosophical and metaphysical nature, and implicit in them is the assumption that they have all 'been written in the years of the plague'.[136] Both plague and cancer were two metaphors for a world in crisis, and Mailer would use them to characterise civilisation's decline into aesthetic squalor, ecological disaster, and iniquitous war and waste. The vision was one of apocalypse – at home, and abroad in Vietnam, with even the haircuts of pop idols being seen as part of a wholesale pessimism:

moonshots fly like flares across black dreams, and the
Beatles – demons or saints? – give shape to a haircut which
looks from the rear like nothing so much as an atomic cloud.
Apocalypse or debauch is upon us. And we are close to
dead . . . the sense of a long last night over civilization is back
again.[137]

Writing a year earlier in 1965, Susan Sontag had also seen the time as 'an age of extremity. For we live under continual threat of two equally fearful, but seemingly opposed, destinies: unremitting banality and inconceivable terror.'[138] Mailer's cultural analysis was similar. As the introduction to *Cannibals and Christians* argues, the terror and the banality are closely related, breeding together 'a world whose ultimate logic is war'. That context was central to his novel *Why Are We in Vietnam?* (1967), and to *The Armies of the Night* (1968), which won both the Pulitzer Prize and the National Book Award.

The Armies of the Night is still, in the view of many, 'his greatest book without any question'.[140] It is a central text of the American 1960s, a book which in Jerry Rubin's words, 'became the bible of the Movement'.[141] Centred upon the anti-Vietnam demonstration which took place at the Pentagon on 21 October 1967, and subtitled 'History as a Novel/The Novel as History', *The Armies of the Night* is probably the finest example of the New Journalism, a form offering an imaginative transfiguration of fact and often placing the journalist-author at the centre of the action. Mailer, in the style of *The Education of Henry Adams*, uses a third-person narrative for an autobiographical account, a technique which would help him achieve his aim, 'to elucidate the mysterious character of that quintessentially American event',[142] the march on the Pentagon. His political analysis insisted on the dynamics of Mystery, which gave the event its generational character. The New Left, or counterculture, had embraced 'the idea of a revolution which preceded ideology'.[143] In the age of the Happening, the Pentagon march was an assault upon a fundamental order:

> politics had again become mysterious, had begun to partake of Mystery: that gave life to a thought the gods were back in

human affairs ... the new generation believed in technology more than any before it, but the generation also believed in LSD, in witches, in tribal knowledge, in orgy, and revolution. It had no respect whatsoever for the unassailable logic of the next step: belief was reserved for the revelatory mystery of the happening where you did not know what was going to happen next; that was what was good about it.[144]

The war in Vietnam is read as a purgation of American neurosis, a neurosis born out of the conflict between technology and Christianity. Mailer endorses the mystery of the spirit at the heart of Christianity, and condemns what he regards as its opposite, the worship of technology. Christianity and the corporation of American business are profound antitheses, and in the effort to reconcile them, America had been driven towards the schizophrenic dissipation of Vietnam:

> He came at last to the saddest conclusion of them all for it went beyond the war in Vietnam. He had come to decide that the centre of America might be insane. The country had been living with a controlled, even fiercely controlled, schizophrenia which had been deepening with the years. ... Any man or woman who was devoutly Christian and worked for the American Corporation, had been caught in an unseen vise whose pressure could split their mind from their soul. For the center of Christianity was a mystery, a son of God, and the center of the corporation was a detestation of mystery, a worship of technology ... the foul brutalities of the war in Vietnam were the only temporary cure possible for the condition – since the expression of brutality offers a definite if temporary relief to the schizophrenic.[145]

Yet *The Armies of the Night* received its acclaim perhaps less for its content than for its formal treatment of that content. Of all the book's reviews, Alfred Kazin's comes closest to gauging its true worth. He proposed a comparison between the book and Walt Whitman's diary of the Civil War, *Specimen Days*, as well as the poet's essay on the crisis of the American Republic during the

Gilded Age, 'Democratic Vistas'. Mailer's *Armies* was worthy of the comparison, wrote Kazin, a work 'that brings to the inner and developing crises of the United States at this moment admirable sensibilities, candid intelligence, the most moving concern for America itself. Mailer's intuition in the book is that the times demand a new form. He has found it.'[146]

Mailer's energetic engagement with the decade's history continued unabated. He finished the 1960s with what still remains the outstanding account of the Apollo moonshot, *Of a Fire on the Moon* (1969), together with his candidacy for mayor of New York. Writing in *Fire*, he proposed a link between his own history and that of the nation – 'a decade so unbalanced in relation to previous American history that Aquarius [Mailer's *nom de plume* in the book], who had begun it by stabbing his second wife in 1960, was to finish by running in a Democratic Primary for Mayor of New York'.[147] For Mailer, the astronauts and the moon landing symbolised the contradictions of the century, and it was this ability to 'contain in their huge contradictions some of the profound and accelerating opposites of the century itself',[148] which gave their endeavour such epic significance. 'Technicians and heroes, robots and saints, adventurers and cogs of the machine'[149] – the Apollo astronauts embodied a complex kind of heroism. Their significance is also couched in terms of metaphysical ambiguity. 'Immediate reflection must tell you that a man who wishes to reach heavenly bodies is an agent of the Lord or Mephisto':[150]

> For the notion that man voyaged out to fulfil the desire of God was either the heart of the vision, or anathema to that true angel in Heaven they would violate by the fires of their ascent. A ship of flames was on its way to the moon.[151]

Mailer's brief in *Fire* is not to offer an account of surfaces, since these are, in the corridors of NASA, as blank as laboratory walls, but rather to seek out occult significances, 'do not dominate this experience with your mind was the lesson – look instead to receive its most secret voice'.[152] This, indeed, is one of the great achievements of this book. In it, Mailer develops a journalism to counter the emptiness of publicity handouts, recognising the need to address the gap between the technological complexities of the Apollo mission, and the human interest stories to do with those involved in the project. Mailer's alternative to this dilemma is to offer his own interpretation of that 'most secret voice'. 'What kind of detective was he, if he could not divine the depths of their character by the depths of his own experience and the few clues the astronauts had already provided in their shielded public interviews?'[153] The book is an impressive achievement, offering both a finely detailed account of the moonshot, its creators and participants, as well as searching out its potential and actual meanings.

The decade was to close with his rather ludicrous bid, on a ticket with Jimmy Breslin, to run for mayor of New York City in the Democratic primary of 1969. According to Hilary Mills's account, Mailer's *naïveté* was obvious in that he was the only one of his team who believed the campaign could succeed. The Mailer–Breslin platform was based on two main notions – New York as fifty-first state of the Union, and giving local political power to individual New York City neighbourhoods. The bid came fourth in a field of five candidates, polling only 41,136 votes, and the campaign says more about Mailer's extraordinary will to carry through ambition than it does about his political wisdom. As the later Jack Abbott scandal was to prove, his instincts were far from sure in the practical universe. He later acknowledged that the mayoralty campaign was profoundly naïve, but only in so far as he had thought 'that people voted as an expression of their desire when he had yet to learn the electorate obtained satisfaction by venting their hate'.[154] Political defeat had left him with, he confessed, 'a huge boredom about himself',[155] the first and last time he would acknowledge that such a state was possible. Yet the year of 1969 also provided national honour with the award of the Pulitzer Prize for *The Armies of the Night*, a more appropriate capstone to a decade of outstanding achievement in American writing. As he entered the 1970s, Mailer considered the possibilities 'and a blank like the windowless walls of the computer city came over his vision ... he had no intimation of what was to come'.[156]

The new decade began with the debate with feminism, or

women's liberation as it was then known. 'Let others beware of receiving the reputation that it is women they do not like',[157] he wrote in *The Prisoner of Sex* (1971), and perhaps his decision that it is 'better to expire as a devil in the fire than an angel in the wings'[158] is one he may regret, for the fires of feminism are still aflame on his reputation in the politically correct 1990s. For those such as Kate Millett and Germaine Greer, Mailer's main offence in the sex wars of the early 1970s was to insist on an existentialist definition of the male and an essentialist principle for the female, whose ultimate expression would always be through the womb. He was, he said at the close of *The Prisoner of Sex*, prepared to accept all the arguments for sexual equality except that one – 'finally, he would agree with everything they asked but to quit the womb'.[159]

The publication of his biography *Marilyn* (1973) brought with it further controversy, with allegations that Mailer had plagiarised the work of two of Marilyn Monroe's biographers, Fred Lawrence Guiles and Maurice Zolotow. The charges were eventually settled and dropped, though as the book's *New York Times* reviewer noted, '*Marilyn* is not a biography at all, it is a meditation on certain biographical facts. Mr Mailer makes it abundantly clear . . . that he depended for the facts of her life on Fred Lawrence Guiles' biography *Norma Jean* and Maurice Zolotow's *Marilyn Monroe*.'[160] Although he had worked in and for Hollywood in the 1950s and developed friendships with such stars as Montgomery Clift and Marlon Brando, who became fixtures at the Mailer salon in those years,[161] he has always maintained that he and Monroe never met. Yet according to Shelley Winters his memory is at fault:

> Contrary to what everybody thinks, contrary to what *he* thinks, he actually met her. Either he doesn't remember or he didn't realize who she was. But Farley Granger saw it happen too, and he remembers it. . . . Marilyn and I had been sharing an apartment on Hollywood Drive . . . I think she may have just done *Asphalt Jungle*. Anyway, we snuck around backstage to see the big movie stars. Norman was backstage, holding a clipboard. He was a kind of stage manager for the rally [in

Introduction: The Shaping of Personality

1948, for the Henry Wallace Presidential campaign].... Then Norman saw us and said 'You're supposed to be out front'. He kicked us out of there and told us to go back out and be ushers – me and Marilyn, both of us. I know Norman doesn't remember, but it's funny, because the whole hype of his Marilyn book was that he'd never met her.[162]

Shelley Winters also remembers how she and Monroe would make up lists of 'the people we'd like to have as lovers', and that Mailer 'was on Marilyn's list. I'm positive.'[163] No doubt Mailer would have enjoyed such appreciation had he been conscious of it, but perhaps the appraisal of a distant film star was necessary to his *Marilyn*, which became 'a triumph of intuitive speculation'.[164] Without any hard evidence, Mailer's book was the first to implicate the Kennedy brothers in Monroe's death, a subject which was to fascinate her biographers throughout the subsequent two decades. His approach was, as he puts it in his introductory chapter 'A Novel Biography', to offer 'a *species* of novel ready to play by the rules of biography'. He gave readers 'a literary hypothesis of a *possible* Marilyn Monroe who might actually have lived and fit most of the facts available. If his instincts were good, then future facts discovered about her would not have to war with the character he created.'[165] Not only were Mailer's instincts good enough to impress in the light of subsequent findings, but as Graham McCann remarks, Mailer is 'in many ways the most "honest" of biographers in his admission of his "novelistic" approach'[166] to his subject. The work remains a powerful interaction between imagination and fact, and transcends the reductive factuality of most Monroe biographies as a result.

The decade would end with one of Mailer's great achievements, the 'true life novel' concerning the life and death of Gary Mark Gilmore, who was executed by firing squad at the Utah State Prison in January 1977. *The Executioner's Song* (1979) is still one of the most original and affecting books to have been written in America in recent years, overextended in parts, but yet in its thousand pages combining a voice and a vision of American life that moves and appalls. Convicted of felony murder, Gilmore demanded that his death sentence be carried out, the first in the United States for ten years, despite appeals against it by groups opposed to capital punishment. As Joan Didion wrote in her review of the book:

> I think no one but Mailer could have dared this book. The authentic Western voice, the voice heard in 'The Executioner's Song', is one heard often in life but only rarely in literature, the reason being that to truly know the West is to lack all will to write it down. The very subject of 'The Executioner's Song' is that vast emptiness at the center of the Western experience, a nihilism antithetical not only to literature but to most other forms of human endeavor, a dread so close to zero that human voices fade out, trail off, like skywriting.[167]

The voice is both medium and message, a meticulously simplified idiom that immediately struck reviewers as absolutely unique in American writing. Mailer himself said he was indebted to his new wife, Barbara Norris Church, for the distinctive 'plains voice' of the narrative. He had met her in 1975, and they were married in 1980, after Mailer divorced his fourth wife, Beverly in 1979. Reviewers of the book were quick to notice the absence of the familiar Mailer voice – 'no gimmicks, no tricks, no *Advertisements for Myself*. The prose is spare and dry and clean. Most important, Mailer does not inject his own personality or judgements into the narrative, doesn't sermonize or philosophize.'[168] Mailer had realised that he had to find a new voice for the 1970s, which would no longer tolerate the high-profile autobiographical style he had used throughout the previous decade. 'The seventies was a period in which we became tremendously fed up with personality', he said, 'and you were just asking to go into the meat grinder if you kept trying to inflict your own personality on to the consciousness of the seventies.'[169] *The Executioner's Song*, along with *The Armies of the Night* and Truman Capote's *In Cold Blood* (1965), is the finest flowering of the New Journalism, a form that uses the design and techniques of fiction to shape history and reportage. Hence the book's subtitle, 'a true

Introduction: The Shaping of Personality 43

life novel', and the decision to award it a Pulitzer Prize for fiction in 1980.

It would, however, be a further three years before Mailer would publish *Ancient Evenings* (1983), his first novel for over twenty-five years. Yet *The Executioner's Song*, which would bring Mailer both commercial and critical acclaim, would also sow the seeds of impending misfortune. In 1977 he had begun a correspondence with Jack Henry Abbott, a convict in Utah State Prison. Abbott had heard that Mailer was at work on the Gary Gilmore case and offered him some first-hand insights into the nature of prison violence. A selection of this correspondence was eventually published in the *New York Review of Books* in 1980, followed in 1981 by the publication of the letters in a book collection titled *In the Belly of the Beast* (1981). This was reviewed by the likes of the *New York Times Book Review*, which reflected the consensus reception in its judgement that Abbott's letters revealed 'an exceptional man with an exceptional literary gift'.[170] The book carried an introduction by Mailer who wrote there of 'all the awe one knows before a phenomenon. Abbott had his own voice. I had heard no other like it.'[171] Although he may not have been responsible for Abbott's early release from prison (which seems to have been as a result of becoming an informant for the prison authorities), Mailer had written a letter to the prison on Abbott's behalf. He was therefore seen by many as guilty by association when, after his release in June 1981, Abbott stabbed and killed a restaurant waiter a few weeks later. Mailer refused to take cover in the subsequent media outrage, eventually testifying on Abbott's behalf when the case came to trial. 'Until all the publicity I hadn't realised people hated Norman as much as they do', his new wife remarked, 'it was a shocking thing to discover – the extent of it.'[172]

This would be the last time Mailer would provoke such frontal public hostility. In the years ahead he continued to publish, with his long awaited 'big book' finally appearing as *Ancient Evenings* in 1983. Along with his most recent novel *Harlot's Ghost* (1991), this will be discussed in the final chapter of this study. In general, however, both these novels seem to suggest Mailer's turn away from polemic, dissent and the American contemporary. In *An-*

cient Evenings the setting is the Egypt of the Pharaohs, and an aspect of the novel's strangeness lies in our sense that the remote milieu has been created by Norman Mailer, whose worlds have always been so pervasively modern, so thoroughly American. And although he returns to the American scene in *Harlot's Ghost*, this too is an historical novel (1956–63), presented more as a chronicle than a critique of its subject, the CIA. Perhaps it is notable that neither novel attempts to engage with the United States since the 1960s. In his recent fiction Mailer has seemed unable or unwilling to enter the age. *Harlot's Ghost* is, to all intents and purposes, an unfinished novel. Though it opens in a time-present of 1983, this rendition of the contemporary is curiously gothic in tone and setting, and Mailer's narrative quickly retreats into the vaults of a Cold War world from which it never surfaces.

At his best, Mailer's real talent resided not in transforming, but in realising the world around him. He would not, could not, deliver that revolution of sensibility he promised in 1959 as the first of his self-promotions, yet he was always determinedly involved in the age, defining its excesses while simultaneously becoming in both his fiction and non-fiction an imaginative witness, charged by the disorders and divisions which were his subject. Yet in the repose of more recent times his writing has offered very little response to the mutations of American culture, in say, the Reagan years. Throughout this period Mailer was looking away, back towards the period featured in *Harlot's Ghost* (1956–63), a retrospect that coincided with his own most convulsive period of self-creating. It is difficult to avoid the conclusion that he has succumbed to the decreativity of repetition, and it may be significant that in his most recent interview he allows that:

> most people, no matter how brilliant, are vessels. Once you come to the end of what is interesting in them, you can touch the side of the jar. There will be nothing afterward but the repetition of what you have learned already. It might take a night, a year, half a lifetime, but once you can reach the side of the vessel, a good part of the larger feeling is gone.[173]

Introduction: The Shaping of Personality

Yet against this decreative repetition must be put the creativity recognised by Susan Sontag, who, writing in 1963, argued that the culture-heroes of that time were 'writers who are repetitive, obsessive, and impolite, who impress by force – not simply by their tone of personal authority and by their intellectual ardor, but by the sense of acute personal and intellectual extremity'.[174] This kind of writing characterises much of Mailer at his most disturbing. He once remarked that this was the highest function of art, precisely that it should disturb, by enlarging experience and by deepening perception. In the best of his fiction we find ourselves involved in an imagination of America tragic, cruel, and sublime, an imagination commensurate with the elaboration of American meaning in the years since 1945.

2
The Hot Breath of the Future:
The Naked and the Dead

'Probably still the best novel about Americans at war, 1941–1945.'[1] So wrote critic Alfred Kazin in 1974 about his subject, Mailer's first published novel, *The Naked and the Dead*. Set on the Pacific island of Anopopei – a fictional setting, though Mailer himself saw action on the Philippine islands of Luzon and Leyte in 1945 – the novel inaugurates some of Mailer's most enduring themes. In its main characters, particularly the American commander, Major General Edward Cummings, and his junior officers Lieutenant Hearn and Sergeant Croft, the reader is forced to consider the pathology of power in a military context as Hearn and Croft lead a reconnaissance platoon on their trek towards Mount Anaka. The novel was a considerable popular and critical success for the young author, and Kazin's judgement of it remains secure today. Power, and its relationship to violence in both the individual and the state, leads to Mailer's first dramatisation of totalitarianism in American life, with Cummings finding in Hitler the 'interpreter of twentieth century man'.[2] The novel's concerns thus extend beyond 'Americans at war, 1941–1945' to address Mailer's fear that with Truman's election in 1945 the United States would emerge from 'the backwaters of history' (321) to inherit its full share in the fascist dream. 'America is going to absorb that dream', says Cummings, 'it's in the business of doing it now' (321).

Diana Trilling was right to feel what she called 'the hot breath of the future' brooding over Mailer's vision in *The Naked and the Dead*.[3] The army world is 'a preview of the future' (324), a microcosm of the political reaction which would threaten the democracies unless a more potent liberal challenge could be developed. But in the novel's political plot the 'bourgeois liberal' Lieutenant Hearn is easily disposed of by both Cummings and Croft, showing the inadequacy of the liberal alternative. However, Mailer's conclusion dramatises his view that the political future belongs not to dangerous mystics like Cummings, but rather to the system's slaves, men like Major Dalleson. He has no wish to transcend the prevailing order, only to be its obedient servant. Fifteen years after the publication of his first novel, in *The Presidential Papers*, Mailer looked back on the intervening decade, the 1950s, years of organisation-man good manners and coercive conformity in American life, years in which the machine mentality of those like Dalleson would flourish: 'America was altered', Mailer wrote, and became 'a vast central swamp of tasteless toneless authority whose dependable heroes were drawn from FBI men, doctors, television entertainers, corporation executives, and athletes who could cooperate with public relations men'.[4] As totalitarianism pervaded almost everything American, it was Dalleson, not Cummings, who epitomised the safe mediocrity of American decline.

Unlike most readers and critics, Mailer is able to see some brighter colours in the bleakness of the novel's tones:

> People say it is a novel without hope. Actually it offers a good deal of hope. I intended it to be a parable about the movement of man through history. I tried to explore the outrageous propositions of cause and effect, of effort and recompense, in a sick society. The book finds man corrupted, confused to the point of helplessness, but it also finds that there are limits beyond which he cannot be pushed, and it finds that even in his corruption and sickness there are yearnings for a better world.[5]

In Mailer's army all are victims, either of each other or of the deterministic trap within which they are boxed almost as soon as they are born. 'My Sam is a mean boy', boasts Jesse Croft of his son, 'I reckon he was whelped mean' (156). In 'The Time Machine' interchapters, we are presented with grim vignettes of American lives in distorted development, and as Jean Radford rightly concludes, 'the result is a systematic indictment of the racialism, sexual neurosis and economic insecurity in American society'.[6] In such conditions idealism does not endure, or if it does, as with Cummings and Croft, it is tainted with inhumanity and contempt for others. 'I HATE EVERYTHING WHICH IS NOT IN MYSELF' is the inner voice screaming from Sam Croft's being. It is difficult to see just where that good deal of hope' exists in this novel's representation of futile striving.

Mailer borrows style and technique from his early literary influences; it is most clearly a first novel in its compliant naturalism, its debts to American novelists of the 1920s and 1930s such as John Steinbeck and John Dos Passos, from whom Mailer took the flashback device of 'The Time Machine':

> I didn't have much literary sophistication while writing *The Naked and the Dead*. I admired Dos Passos immensely and wanted to write a book that would be like one of his. My novel was frankly derivative, directly derivative . . . I had four books on my desk all the time I was writing: *Anna Karenina, Of Time and the River, U.S.A.*, and *Studs Lonigan*. . . . The atmosphere of *The Naked and the Dead*, the overspirit, is Tolstoyan; the rococo comes out of Dos Passos; the fundamental, slogging style from Farrell, and the occasional overrich descriptions from Wolfe.[7]

In his reliance upon such models, Mailer demonstrated for the first and last time in his writing career an 'all-bets-covered caution'[8] with respect to the form his novel took. Critics have also been quick to point out the political and philosophical correspondences between the novel and its antecedents in the leftist American literary scene of the 1930s. In its stress upon deterministic views of human behaviour, and its realisation of a world in which the individual is dehumanised and subjected to the efficient functioning of entrenched systems of control, *The Naked and the Dead* may seem a somewhat stale recapitulation of a vision and a style inappropriate to a changed postwar world. However, as Nigel Leigh has argued, one should not be misled by the novel's dated style since Mailer's concern is not primarily retrospective, 'not a historical preoccupation with the war itself', but is rather prophetic, to do with 'the crises of the post-war United States'.[9]

In the shadow of the Holocaust, Mailer, like Saul Bellow, a Jewish-American contemporary whose first novel, *Dangling Man*, appeared in 1944, saw America's future, humanity's future, as tending towards the cancellation of freedom and creative individualism. There are intriguing similarities to be found in these first novels by two writers who were to dominate American literature in the post-war period. Both Bellow and Mailer conclude their novels ironically; the war fought for freedom and democracy has somehow contrived to undermine the appeal of these ideals, and in Bellow's novel we see his central character, Joseph, fleeing freedom and self-consciousness to embrace the regimentation of the Army. In view of Mailer's later exaltation of 'American existentialism' in the figure of the hipster, it is also interesting that at the end of the narrative Joseph is what might be termed an exhausted existentialist who has found freedom to be disabling. 'To be pushed upon oneself entirely put the very facts of simple existence in doubt',[10] he concludes. With underscored irony Bellow presents his character as an existential failure, deep in the bad faith of his gratitude that with the Army to save him he would no longer 'be held accountable' for himself; he is willing to explore the route down which Mailer's broken soldiers go, to open himself to war's means – 'perhaps the war could teach me, by violence, what I had been unable to learn during those months in the room'.[11] In both novels, then, we witness the demise of liberal humanism as it succumbs to the leash of military structure. The efforts of individuals to reach their goals end in defeat. Croft fails to lead his platoon to the summit of Mount Anaka – 'he had failed, and it hurt him vitally' (709), while Cummings's strategy to breach the Toyaku line from Botoi Bay is overtaken by Dalleson's unplanned breakthrough overland. The latter's emergence as mock-hero looks forward to many such types in that other, rather delayed American novel of the Second World War, Joseph Heller's *Catch-22*, where again we see the military as a paradigm of inhuman totalitarian bureaucracy.

Both Heller and Mailer, like Hemingway before them, offer us war as a metaphor for much else besides. In its structures and effects on men it represents Mailer's view of the modern social order. As Richard Poirier has noted, '"war" was the determining form of his imagination long before he had the direct experiences of war that went into his first big novel'.[12] Yet if war was the specific and figurative context of *The Naked and the Dead*, the novel has very little to say about the military enemy, the Japanese, whose forces, led by General Toyaku, the Americans need to overcome if they are to take Anopopei. As Leigh remarks, 'no attempt is made to write about the international nature of the war: there are few allusions to Japan (the single Japanese character, Wakara, is given only a few pages); Germany and Italy are merely mentioned in passing'. Mailer is concerned 'with the enemy located within . . . the United States'.[13] As we become more familiar with the platoon members we find that what they most despise and fear is rooted in their prior experience of life in America. As mentioned previously, in 'The Time Machine' Mailer cuts a cross-section of American life and finds there the ugly reality behind the American Dream of success and fulfilment. 'No Apple Pie Today' is the title of Brown's 'Time Machine' chapter, and soon enough he and his colleagues learn to give up on deferred dreams, and to hope instead for a minimal survival. As Red Valsen knows,

> You carried it alone as long as you could, and then you weren't strong enough to take it any longer. You kept fighting everything, and everything broke you down, until in the end you were just a little goddamn bolt holding on and squealing when the machine went too fast. (703–4)

In Lieutenant Hearn's view, only General Cummings seemed capable of transcending what he calls 'the busy complex mangle, the choked vacuum of American life' (85). This is the America out of which Mailer's soldiers struggle. In contrast to it the Army may even have its attractions – order, a certain place in the hierarchy, and the hope, however baseless, that soldiering would not be without its satisfactions. On board the landing craft taking them back from Mount Anaka the platoon members found 'a startled pride in themselves . . . "we did okay to go as far as we did"' (708). Against this Mailer puts the America of 'The Time Machine', one that chokes and mangles individual effort, an ironic reverse of the mythical land of untrammelled possibility, the Dream America.

Much of the critical commentary on *The Naked and the Dead* has focused upon the problematic relationship between the novel's critique of totalitarianism and Mailer's representation of the fascist mentality. Readers are right to see the novel as an extensive political allegory through which Mailer dramatises for the first time in fiction his enduring belief that America is being destroyed by totalitarianism. The difficulties arise when we begin to consider Mailer's characters and the extent to which they embody this political vision. Cummings, Croft and Hearn have often been cast as the main players in an ideological war:

> The central conflict in *The Naked and the Dead* is between the mechanistic forces of 'the system' and the will to individual integrity. Commanding General Cummings, brilliant and ruthless evangel of fascist power and control, and ironhanded, hard-nosed Sergeant Croft personify the machine.[14]

Against these is ranged the 'confused humanism'[15] of Lieutenant Hearn. The problem with this interpretation, as some critics have seen, is that by its logic Cummings and Croft ought to emerge as victors. Yet while it is true that Hearn is unequivocally defeated, effectively murdered by both men, so too both Cummings and Croft are defeated, their individual will to conquer undermined by the absurdities of chance (Croft and his platoon run in panic from a swarm of hornets, when Croft kicks over their nest accidentally; Cummings's plan to outflank the Toyaku line is thwarted by Dalleson's success, which is achieved by accident rather than by design). This conclusion is problematic for those who take the view that Cummings and Croft embody totalitarian values – as creatures of the system their survival would be expected so as to stress Mailer's belief in its hegemony. Instead, the novel's ending appears to confound such expectations:

> The conclusion ... and its total meaning are unclear. The failure of Cummings' and Croft's designs would seem to indicate the failure of the machine to work its will upon man and nature, and to justify reading the novel as a 'parable' of man's refusal to be dehumanized by the forces of mechanized society. Yet Hearn's death and Valsen's shattering humiliation clearly dramatize the defeat of man by the machine.[16]

The flaw in such a reading lies in its assumption that Cummings and Croft simplistically embody the machine mentality of totalitarianism. In *The Presidential Papers*, Mailer confessed to having had a 'secret admiration' for characters like Sam Croft – 'behind the ideology in *The Naked and the Dead* was an obsession with violence. The characters for whom I had the most secret admiration, like Croft, were violent people'. While it is true that Croft shares with Cummings much that is evil – he is for the most part inhumane in his dealings with others, and like Cummings, he can kill easily and with relish, he yet possesses certain qualities which make him an enemy, rather than a servant of a totalitarian system. Cummings and Croft, so far from being outright villains, can even be seen as the novel's natural heroes. They are both self-exalting, both visionaries who would impose themselves upon the world. As Nigel Leigh has argued, 'seen as the only source of vitalist power in a naturalistic world, they are not without an heroic dimension ... Cummings and Croft possess a charisma absent from all the other characters'.[17] For Robert Solotaroff, Croft is still 'after four subsequent novels, the most compelling character by far that Mailer has created', and he sees him as 'the novel's true idealist'.[18] Richard Gilman is another critic who argues that 'Mailer was clearly more ravished than a programmatically humanist writer would have been by the ostensible villains of his tale'.[19]

If Cummings and Croft are indeed Mailer's crypto-heroes, we

need to consider their relationship to the unquestionable demon of the novel, totalitarianism. To what extent *do* they 'personify the machine'? Mailer's first extended definition of totalitarianism came in 'The Ninth Presidential Paper'. There, he argues that the most insidious aspect of it is that 'it beheads individuality, variety, dissent, extreme possibility, romantic faith, it blinds vision, deadens instinct, it obliterates the past'.[20] In political and social terms, totalitarianism cannot tolerate those who demand to express themselves independently of the system. As a result it produces a culture marked by mediocrity, conformity and the elimination of any human aspiration except as that serves the system. 'It would be the hacks who would occupy history's seat after the war' (718) thinks Cummings ruefully. At the end of the novel Mailer leaves us with Dalleson and his big idea:

> He could jazz up the map-reading class by having a full-size color photograph of Betty Grable in a bathing suit, with a co-ordinate grid system laid over it. The instructor could point to different parts of her and say, 'Give me the co-ordinates.' Goddamn, what an idea! (721)

In Mailer's view, totalitarianism rewards hacks, not heroes. In his next novel, *Barbary Shore*, Mailer's first-person narrator, Lovett, says, 'it's a measure of the disaster that everywhere the bureaucrat has the magic power'. And in *An American Dream* Barney Kelley reinforces the point for Steve Rojack, telling him 'it's the hard-working fellow at the desk who has the real power'. Cummings, for all his insights into the military mind, is blind to his own logic. He tells Hearn that 'in the Army the idea of individual personality is just a hindrance' (180–1), yet fails to see that his own arrogant, even demiurgic personality ('You know, if there is a God, Robert, he's just like me' – 183) may be a touch more than the Army can stand. It is important to see that in Cummings's politics, Mailer has domesticated fascism, mobilising its appeal from a European to an American context. As Jean Radford has noted, Cummings's 'is "a peculiarly American" brand of fascism, combining individualism and idealism with a dream of totalitarianism'.[21]

Through such characterisations, Mailer shows that one of the side-roads from the transcendentalist celebration of the self leads to a fascist view of man. It is a short step from Whitman's 'I celebrate myself' to Croft's 'I hate everything which is not in myself'. Cummings believes that man is naturally fascist, and that in Hitler was 'the interpreter of twentieth-century man' (313). However, at the end of *The Naked and the Dead*, Mailer's concern with American capitalism and fascism has shifted to focus instead on the dangers of totalitarianism. In his study of Mailer, Joseph Wenke discriminates between the developing stages of totalitarianism and their treatment of idiosyncratic personality:

> For there is a species of revolution and counterrevolution within totalitarianism itself. Though a totalitarian movement may well have its origin in a powerful and charismatic personality committed to risktaking as a means of achieving power, totalitarian institutions gravitate inexorably toward a consolidation of power and an elimination of personality.[22]

For all that must be said against the fascist disposition of Cummings or Croft, both men possess qualities which fly in the face of the machine mentality. Mailer has said that Melville's *Moby Dick* was 'the biggest influence'[23] on *Naked*, and certainly one can see resemblances between the vaunting ambitions of Captain Ahab and those of General Cummings. Both men are solitary, mystical, fastened to their omnipotent urges:

> Always, he had had to be alone, he had chosen it that way, and he would not renege now, nor did he want to . . . Cummings stared at the vast dark bulk of Mount Anaka, visible in the darkness as a deeper shadow, a greater mass than the sky above it. It was the axis of the island, its keystone. There's an affinity, he told himself. If one wanted to get mystical about it, the mountain and he understood each other. Both of them, from necessity, were bleak and alone, commanding the heights. (563)

Cummings does not regard himself as a functionary of the military system, rather as standing outside its means; his ultimate goal is superhuman, to take charge of his island world, to subdue 'whatever lay between Hearn and himself, between himself and the five thousand troops against him, the terrain, and the circuits of chance he would mold' (85). Like Ahab, Cummings tests himself against considerable adversaries; and like Ahab he is finally defeated in his aims. Chance, in the shape of Major Dalleson, defeats him; and so too do his troops who 'resisted him, resisted change, with maddening inertia. No matter how you pushed them, they always gave ground sullenly, regrouped once the pressure was off . . . there were times now when he doubted basically whether he could change them, really mold them' (717). Victory over the Japanese, which might have been accomplished by his own grand plan was, he is forced to concede, 'accomplished by a random play of vulgar good luck' (716).

Nevertheless, though both Cummings and Croft fail, their failures are redeemed by heroism. In Mailer's terms, they refuse to be trapped in the conventions of the military machine; they are each examples of extreme individualism, resisting the system's imperative of efficiency. Croft's obsessive desire to scale Mount Anaka has, in the end, no military justification whatsoever; and Cummings's plan to accelerate the Japanese defeat by launching an invasion by the sea route of Botoi Bay involves unnecessary risk, expense (since it can only be carried out with additional naval support), and, more than this, it is conceived not to serve the system but primarily to glorify Major-General Edward Cummings. 'What a conception it was', Cummings congratulates himself, 'there was an unorthodoxy, a daring about it, which appealed to him greatly' (399). He has an intellectual contempt for the officer class, and despises the 'hacks' at GHQ on whom he nevertheless has to depend. With several carefully chosen images, Mailer finally establishes Cummings not as an uncritical agent of, but as a threat to the machine mentality to which he feels superior. In the following passage Cummings reacts to the news that his troops have been gaining ground in a slow advance on the Toyaku line; although this is achieving the military objective, it also threatens Cummings's more flamboyant Botoi Bay plan:

> All day as he had sat in the operations tent, reading the reports that had come in, he had been a little annoyed. He had felt like a politician on election night, he thought, who was watching the party candidate win and feeling chagrined because he had tried to nominate another man. The damn thing was unimaginative, stale, any commander could have mounted it successfully, and it would be galling to admit that the Army was right. (561)

It is very clear that Cummings regards himself as specially gifted, superior to the dull efficiencies of the military machine. This impression is consolidated in another image – where Mailer stresses that for Cummings, the strategies of war imply a creative effort. For victory must carry a personal signature. He is not willing to be a machine operative: 'Cummings was bothered by a suspicion, very faint, not quite stated, that he had no more to do with the success of the attack than a man who presses a button and waits for the elevator' (560).

So, although Cummings is undoubtedly fascistic in his views, he is yet, by nature, an enemy of totalitarianism, which would in Mailer's terms 'behead' his kind of aggressive individualism. As for Sergeant Croft, who in many ways shares Cummings's faults, there would be reincarnation of sorts in Mailer's urban frontiersman, the white negro. As many critics have noted, Croft is in significant ways the prototype of this figure. A psychopath who 'smouldered with an endless hatred' (164), he yet personifies much that is essential to Mailer's 'philosophical psychopath' in the violent radicalism he would advocate a decade later. In his important essay of 1960, 'Superman Comes to the Supermarket', Mailer would trace what he called the 'psychotization' of America back to its frontier history. In a compelling piece of cultural analysis he saw twentieth-century American history as almost fatally split between 'two rivers':

> one visible, the other underground; there has been the history of politics which is concrete, factual, practical and unbelievably dull . . . and there is a subterranean river of untapped,

ferocious, lonely and romantic desires, that concentration of ecstasy and violence which is the dream life of the nation.[24]

Croft exemplifies this cultural disjunction. His 'Time Machine' narrative tells us of his violent upbringing, explicitly tied to the raw aggression of frontier-breaking ancestors. His father, who literally beats his values into his son, is proud of the issue:

> 'He got good stock in him' Jesse Croft declared to his neighbours. 'We was one of the first folks to push in here, must be sixty years ago, and they was Crofts in Texas over a hunnerd years ago. Ah'd guess some of them had that same meanness that Sam's got. Maybe it was what made 'em push down here.' (15)

Like Cummings, Croft's nature subverts crucial features of the totalitarianism which Mailer abhors, and as such, Croft also acquires some degree of heroism in the narrative. His urges are irrational, instinctive, influenced by the pull of blood from a primitive ancestry; he too owns his ancestors' meanness, their frontiering drive to 'push down' and 'push in' to new, unknown territory. As Solotaroff notes, Croft's violence is atavistic:

> as the prototype of the hipster, Croft instinctively knows what actions will minister to his ailments and enable him to break open the walls which have held his straining psyche encased. Anaka contains within its bulk all the frontiers that have been closed to Croft.[25]

Totalitarianism, which 'deadens instinct' and 'obliterates the past', would certainly regard Croft's type as tending to undermine its objectives. Nigel Leigh has argued that Croft cannot be described as either totalitarian or fascist:

> He is clearly outside the political categories. Although his nature is decidedly non-liberal . . . in a number of ways he is notably non-fascistic: he has no connection with groups on the American right, as might be expected; he is less racist, ethno-

centric or anti-Semitic than most of the working-class men in his command; and he is the only person to show affection for the Mexican Martinez.[26]

Neither Leigh nor the other critics quoted in this discussion underestimate the capacity for evil in Cummings and Croft; while resisting the mechanistic efficiencies of the military as tending to degrade his own potentialities, Cummings nevertheless advocates such a reductive standard for most of the rest of humanity. Both he and Croft exemplify the iniquitous relationship between violence and power. Listening to the sounds of war, Cummings experiences a sense of erotic exaltation:

> The war, or rather, *war*, was odd, he told himself . . . it was all covered with tedium and routine, regulations and procedure, and yet there was a naked quivering heart to it which involved you deeply when you were thrust into it. All the deep dark urges of man, the sacrifices on the hilltop, and the churning lusts of the night and sleep, weren't all of them contained in the shattering screaming burst of a shell, the man-made thunder and light? . . . All of it, all the violence, the dark coordination had sprung from his mind. In the night, at that moment, he felt such power that it was beyond joy. (566–7)

As Richard Poirier noted, in *The Naked and the Dead*, Mailer had 'not yet learned how to suggest any possible heroic resistance to the encroaching forces of totalitarianism',[27] for even though it has been possible to point up manifestations of heroism in Cummings and Croft, this is unquestionably heroism of a very problematic kind. As Joseph Wenke has argued, the novel 'sets Mailer's talent for creating powerful and violent characters at odds with the thematic necessity of placing some limits on the success of totalitarians'.[28] Yet if, as Wenke writes, Cummings and Croft 'prove to be the novel's most dynamic characters',[29] this is mainly due to the weakness of their opposition, provided in the shape of Lieutenant Hearn. Although Hearn is often seen as his spokesman, Mailer has referred to Hearn as 'a despised image of myself'.[30] The author's friends recall that after publication of the novel, he seemed more drawn to Croft's character – 'we'd all read *The Naked and the Dead* in galleys. I'm sure of this, because when we took our trip to Mont-Saint-Michel we were already playing a game called "The Naked and the Dead." Bea was usually Wilson, and Norman always wanted to be Croft.'[31] The image of Mailer 'doing Croft . . . running around yelling, bullying'[32] and shouting in a Croft-like southern accent on a beach near Mont-Saint-Michel is not prepossessing, except that it may confirm his natural dislike of the officer mentality represented by Hearn. 'The hatred of officers went over to the minor characters, the minor officers', he has said.[33] Creating Croft's character in the novel 'came naturally . . . but Hearn and Cummings drove me crazy'.[34]

Nigel Leigh provides one of the best studies of Hearn's role in the novel's structures, both thematic and technical. With regard to the latter, Leigh notes that:

> In the unfolding narrative Hearn cements the disparate elements of the book together and remains the only character rendered with both realistic authority and psychological depth. He provides the nearest thing in the text to a constant point of view. . . . His world view provides a positive point of resistance to the fascism of Cummings and Croft and to power in a much more generalized sense.[35]

He contends that Hearn 'not only represents a broad inclination towards Marxist values but also carries much of Mailer's personality' and then advances the unusual proposition that Mailer's connection with Hearn 'is coded in the text through Hearn's peculiar role as a Jew'.[36] Hearn, of course, is not Jewish, but rather a WASP. Still, Leigh argues that Mailer's portrait of Hearn as a 'pseudo-Jew' is consistent with the author's own unwillingness to be closely identified with a Jewish sensibility. As noted above, he has acknowledged Hearn as 'some extension of myself, a despised image of myself', and Leigh's remarks may consolidate Leslie Fiedler's assessment of Mailer as in many respects an 'anti-Jew'.[37] But if Hearn can be described as a pseudo-Jew, suggesting Mailer's own ambivalence with regard to ethnic identity, so too can he be described as a pseudo-liberal. His political affiliations are the cause of some critical disagreement. While many are content to describe Hearn as a liberal, Leigh stresses that he should certainly be seen as 'a radical liberal', while Robert Merrill believes that 'Hearn does not so much represent liberalism as the *desire* to be liberal . . . temperamentally, Hearn is an aristocrat'.[38] I cannot agree with those critics who regard Hearn as an effective counterforce to the values represented by Cummings or Croft, for Hearn's liberalism is often seen to be a soft target, easily collapsing in the face of Cummings's theoretical rigour, and proving no match for Croft's manic single-mindedness. Far from having created in Hearn a force that can 'counteract the personal and political excesses of the other two major characters', one who 'provides a positive point of resistance to the fascism of Cummings and Croft',[39] the overwhelming impression for me is of a man without stable convictions. When in Cummings's orbit, Hearn feels himself to be 'basically like Cummings . . . they were both the same' (392); when in Croft's presence, Hearn realises he has to leave since 'if he stayed he would become another Croft' (586). So while Leigh is correct to say that with Hearn's death 'the most enlightened position in the novel has been shown to be insubstantial', this is due to more than 'the conspiracy of values between Cummings and Croft'.[40] As their ideological opponent, Hearn fails to convince because as a character he lacks those qualities Mailer has always deemed admirable. When he looks at Mount Anaka, all he can see is an image of defeat – 'it was the kind of shore upon which huge ships would founder, smash apart, and sink in a few minutes' (498). In contrast to Hearn's 'fear' of the mountain, Croft in looking at its bulk is exalted by its beauty – 'the mountain and the cloud and the sky were purer, more intense, in their gelid silent struggle than any ocean and any shore he had ever seen' (497). Had Mailer been fully behind Hearn's politics he would have surely sought out the kind of objective correlative which Anaka provides in Croft's case. Instead we have in Hearn a feeble ideologue whose final decision is to retire from the struggle, to resign his commission.

The most astute analysis of Mailer's politics in *The Naked and*

The Hot Breath of the Future 61

the Dead is still that offered by Norman Podhoretz in 1959. For Podhoretz, the novel shows Mailer discovering 'that American liberalism is bankrupt' because:

> it is animated by a vision of the world that neither calls forth heroic activity nor values the qualities of courage, daring, and will that make for the expansion of the human spirit . . . ultimately what Mailer was looking for – and has continued to look for – is not so much a more equitable world as a more exciting one, a world that produces men of size and a life of huge possibility, and this was nowhere to be found in the kind of liberalism to which he committed himself in the earliest phase of his literary career.[41]

In his first novel Mailer represented war as an incubator of totalitarianism in American life. In his next, *Barbary Shore*, American idealism is all but gone, replaced by the cold grip of political reaction.

3

Ambush in the Alley: *Barbary Shore* and *The Deer Park*

Robert Merrill, the author of a book-length study of Mailer's work, offers a comprehensive analysis of that work with one outstanding exception. The reader searching for a chapter, or even a section of a chapter on *Barbary Shore* would find that Merrill simply dismisses Mailer's second novel as a 'miserable failure'.[1] Merrill cites Mailer's remarks on *Barbary Shore* in *Advertisements for Myself*, where he makes his appeal to posterity – 'it could be that if my work is alive one hundred years from now, *Barbary Shore* will be considered the richest of my first three novels'.[2] To which Merrill responds, 'Let us hope not.'[3] Others have been just as clear in their condemnation. Richard Gilman tells us that the novel is 'hopelessly bad, ponderously written, confused, uncertain of what it wants to do, unconvincing in its structure and its imaginative premises'.[4] Critics who choose other terms with which to judge it seem to be reaching for euphemisms, referring to its 'transitional nature',[5] or to its giving readers 'moments of intellectual sharpness in a world that is novelistically flat'.[6] Some have found *Barbary Shore* well-nigh unreadable. Robert Solotaroff finds that 'it grows steadily more choked and claustral. One has to struggle to get through the last forty pages.'[7] Still, as Marvin Mudrick noted, the novel does at least have 'the crude look of chance-taking and exploration',[8] and although in the final analysis it is a poor novel, from today's vantage point it can be regarded as a key to Mailer's development as he struggled to find a style and a politics of his own. In his interviews Mailer has always traced the novel's confusion and thematic instability to such origins:

> *Barbary Shore* was built on the division which existed then in my mind. My conscious intelligence . . . became obsessed by the Russian Revolution. But my unconscious was much more interested in other matters: murder, suicide, orgy, psychosis, all the themes I discuss in *Advertisements*. Since the gulf between these conscious and unconscious themes was vast and quite resistant to any quick literary coupling, the tension to get a bridge across resulted in the peculiar hothouse atmosphere of the book. My unconscious felt one kind of dread, my conscious mind another, and *Barbary Shore* lives somewhere in between. That's why its focus is so unearthly.[9]

As an evocation of the American socio-political atmosphere in the 1950s the novel is at points almost definitive, an early indication of Mailer's sensitivity to the reality beneath appearances. As Richard Poirier has written, it contains 'passages of lurid, startling brilliance',[10] the most memorable of which convey the underside to that well-adjusted Cold War patriotism of the age. The vision of the novel is of an America in barbary, where morality and politics are epitomised by the depravity of Leroy Hollingsworth, a secret policeman with 'a mind like a garbage pail'. In Solotaroff's words, what:

> emerges from the unconscious in *Barbary Shore*'s allegorical rendering of psychic America are feelings of aggression, narcissism, guilt and terror which find expression in the sadism, masochism, nymphomania, homosexuality, hysteria, and near insanity which fills the novel.[11]

'Few people who like my work have read it, and yet much of my later writing cannot be understood without a glimpse of the odd shadow and theme-maddened light *Barbary Shore* casts before it.'[12] So wrote Mailer in the 'Second Advertisement for Myself'. This was as true in 1959 as today, when in the aftermath of his most recent novel, *Harlot's Ghost*, we can see that this novel of the CIA had its first seeds planted in the character of Hollingsworth and the related ambience of spying, masquerade and betrayal which afflicts all those who live in the Brooklyn rooming-house of *Barbary Shore*. Mailer described the novel as his 'most autobiographical' and in the character of Michael Lovett, the narrator, we have a projection of Mailer's changing self as he moved away from the political activism of the late 1940s to explore the radical individualism which would issue forth in 'The White Negro' essay of 1957. Mailer referred to the novel as 'this first of the existentialist novels in America',[13] and again Lovett is to some extent a prototype for the hipster as existential hero. Due to his amnesia Lovett is forced to live in the present, an essential feature of the hipster's reality as defined in 'The White Negro'. As a man who 'had no past and was therefore without a future' (4), Lovett occupies a position very similar to Mailer's own. After the success of *The Naked and the Dead*, he was forced to explore the unknown self, and the experience of writing *Barbary Shore* was existentially formative:

> Success had been a lobotomy to my past, there seemed no power from the past which could help me in the present, and I had no choice but to force myself to step into the war of the enormous present, to accept the private heat and fatigue of setting out by myself to cut a track through a new world. . . . *Barbary Shore* was really a book to emerge from the bombarded cellars of my unconscious, an agonized eye of a novel which tried to find some amalgam of my new experience and the larger horror of that world which might be preparing to destroy itself.[14]

Mailer thus casts himself as an existential pioneer, the self outside history, destitute of political idealism, but a philosophical missionary whose purpose is desperate: to create individual possibility where collective will has failed. This too is Lovett's position at the end of *Barbary Shore*. As the inheritor of McLeod's unnamed 'little object', which we can surmise to be the residue of a socialist humanism, a hope for man, Lovett is a member of 'a new generation with new strength' (245). He tells us that as a result of being a fugitive, his experience has been provisional, dislocated, set against the threat of mass destruction – 'if I fled down the alley which led from that rooming house, it was only to enter another, and then another. I am obliged to live waiting for the signs which tell me I must move on again. . . . Meanwhile, vast armies mount themselves . . . the march to the endless war forces its pace' (311). The imagery used here is very similar to that used in Mailer's confession above, as is Lovett's more hopeful summary of having stepped into his own war of 'the enormous present' – 'I have come to understand the skeleton perhaps of that larger history, and not everything is without its purpose. I have even achieved a balance' (5). Lovett's 'balance' reflects Mailer's 'amalgam' of self and world and is assuredly one index to this novel's 'most autobiographical' context. In such ways *Barbary Shore* is a highly personal document. It may have had the appearance of being a good deal less rooted in his own experience than *Naked*, whereas in fact the opposite was the case. Much more than damaged ego was involved in his recoil from the reviewers' sting (in *Advertisements*, he referred to *Barbary Shore* as having been 'ambushed in the alley' by its reviewers), for the novel was born out of his deepest self, and his reaction to its bloody beating by the critics is that of parent to child as he wrote of the novel's being 'torn from its expected reception and given a shrunken life which was to react on the life of the author and reduce him as well'.[15] More than his novel, it was Norman Mailer whose defects were being ridiculed.

Set in a Brooklyn rooming-house, the novel's historical context is that of a war turned from hot to cold. As in his first novel, here Mailer again makes use of the social microcosm, with Croft's war-weary platoon becoming the post-war cross-section of Michael Lovett, three other roomers – Hollingsworth, McLeod and Lannie – along with the landlady Guinevere and her daughter Monina, representing American society. The concept of the rooming-house allowed Mailer to suggest much about the relationship between individuals and between individuals and the state in post-war America. At the close of *The Naked and the Dead* Mailer gave us Major Dalleson as the epitome of the bureaucratic mentality which would control the political future. As Nigel Leigh reminds us, 'the repressed, compartmentalized personality structure of the bureaucrat is neurotic. Guilt, fears of persecution and sexual chaos are concealed from public view.'[16] In Mailer's vision America is a rooming-house, an establishment of distant corridors and empty rooms. Isolation, alienation and a clammy fear of the enemies both within and without give rise to distorted lives. Inside, the inhabitants exist in their compartments, hiding from their truest selves. Lovett, our guide and narrator, has taken a room so that he can finish a novel, a novel most appropriately concerned with a nameless, faceless institution. Alone among the characters in *Barbary Shore*, Lovett has creative ambition, has the self-discipline and willpower to express himself creatively. He tells us he 'was driven with the ambition to be a writer' and that his 'project was to save five hundred dollars and then find an inexpensive room' (7). And so eventually, though the kindness of a playwright friend, he makes his first approach to the rooming-house:

> It was a big house and gave the impression of being an empty house. Downstairs there were ten names arranged in ten brackets next to as many bells which did not ring, but a week could go by and I would pass no one upon the stairs. I hardly cared. In the last months I had come to know fewer and fewer people . . . for better or for worse I was very much alone. (19)

Lovett is also isolated from himself by an amnesia which is almost total, probably the result of a war wound. His meetings with the landlady Beverly Guinevere, her husband McLeod, and fellow roomers Hollingsworth and Lannie Madison will comprise almost all the history he has. He is, then, something of an innocent, and his narrative consists of a series of encounters which collectively supply his education for life in post-war America. That Mailer intends Lovett's experiences to be typical of that life is indicated in the final chapter where he tells us that 'if I fled down the alley which led from that rooming-house, it was only to enter another, and then another' (311).

Many critics have read *Barbary Shore* as a political allegory, with a Manichean struggle under way between the forces of light and dark. Lovett is both a witness to and, ultimately, the most significant participant in this war, which has McLeod, the worn-out revolutionary, being interrogated and eventually murdered by secret policeman Hollingsworth. McLeod's wife, Guinevere (surely one of the most implausible nuptials in all American fiction), is thought to represent the masses in terms of the political allegory, while Lannie Madison has been a follower of Trotsky, a position with which Lovett too has some sympathy. According to John Stark, 'the changing alliances and rivalries, the successes and failures in the novel allegorically present a capsule history of the Left',[17] while Diana Trilling, in one of the first discussions of the novel, argues that 'as Mailer's highly allegorical story progresses, it turns out that this secret of our future rehabilitation is never recaptured by Hollingsworth, but the dark powers of reaction are nonetheless triumphant'.[18] Other critics have found it more difficult to treat the novel as an allegory. For Robert Ehrlich 'the shifting allegiances of the complex characters make it questionable to call Lovett the Trotskyist, and Hollingsworth the fascist. . . . *Barbary Shore* possesses too much density to allow for the easy definitions of political allegory.'[19]

If *Barbary Shore* fails as a novel, one of the main reasons is that its allegory is confused. Readers are never given the allegory's coordinates clearly enough; without this an essential prerequisite of allegory is missing. It is perhaps for this reason that the most memorable character in the novel is that of Leroy Hollingsworth; he, at least, we know to be thoroughly iniquitous. On the other hand, his main adversary, McLeod, is ideologically unstable, something of a quisling whose record with the Communists has included taking part in political assassinations as an agent of the Stalinist purges. Lannie vilifies him as 'the undertaker of the revolution' (187). He has since quit the Communist Party after the signing of the Nazi–Soviet pact, and has been working for the American government. To incorporate him into an allegorical plot as 'the Bolshevist McLeod'[20] is to oversimplify, though for the allegory to succeed McLeod needed to be as clearly valorised as Hollingsworth. As with *The Naked and the Dead*, where the characterisation of liberal virtue in Hearn is weakly drawn in comparison to its charismatic eclipse by the fascist power of both Croft and Cummings, so in *Barbary Shore* it is clear that Mailer's pull was at least ambiguous, with Hollingsworth in ascendancy. In the 'Third Advertisement for Myself', he writes of his sense that his second novel had a subtext to it which was very much out of step with the times. As opposed to 'the worship of the lifeless, the senseless, and the safe' in 1950s America, his own deepest impulse 'was leading toward the violent and the orgiastic':

> I do not mean that I was clear about where I was going, it was rather that I had a dumb dull set of intimations that the things I was drawn to write about were taboo ... the direction I took in *Barbary Shore* was a step toward work I will probably be doing from now on. For I wish to attempt an entrance into the mysteries of murder, suicide, incest, orgy, orgasm, and Time.[21]

In 'the peculiar hothouse atmosphere' of the novel, it is significant that Mailer uses Hollingsworth's perverted sexuality as a major sign of his corruption. He is, as McLeod tells Lovett, 'a pretty sick individual', 'a madman' (36). After the appearance of *An American Dream* Mailer was to become demonised by feminists such as Kate Millett, who used some very dubious 'close readings' of that novel to make the case for his being misogynistic. It is regrettable that those such as Millett could not have been more thorough, since in *Barbary Shore*, male sexual violence is condemned quite unequivocally. In Hollingsworth we see the true horror of fascism unleashed in his perversion of love into sadism:

he proceeded to tell her how he loved her, his speech containing more obscenity than I had ever heard in so short a space, and in rapid succession . . . he named various parts of her body and described what he would do to them, how he would tear this and squeeze that, eat here and spit there, butcher rough and slice fine, slash, macerate, pillage, all in an unrecognizable voice which must have issued between clenched teeth. (203)

This character's 'sadistic and obscene authoritarianism',[22] his position as the novel's ugliest image of 'mankind in barbary' is unmistakeably conveyed by way of his covert and malign sexual imagination, a fact that ought to have been considered by any critic offering a considered account of sexual ethics in Mailer's work as a whole.

Most critics have seen the parallels between Hollingsworth and those characters who contested the route to future power in *The Naked and the Dead*. For John Stark, Hollingsworth is 'a false liberal like the ones that Mailer warned about at the end of *The Naked and the Dead*, a weaker, less impressive, more clearly evil enemy than Cummings'.[23] Although Jean Radford describes Hollingsworth, rather oddly, as the novel's 'anti-hero', she too sees that he 'embodies some of the qualities of Croft and Cummings along with the role and sensibilities of Major Dalleson'.[24] Nigel Leigh agrees with Radford, while unaccountably criticising her for having missed Hollingsworth's 'real affinity with Major Dalleson'.[25]

At the end of the novel, Hollingsworth's further dominance is established as both Guinevere and Lannie turn to him for a share in a possible future. It is Guinevere who suggests that she and Hollingsworth escape 'to the ends of the earth. To Barbary' (205). Both she and Lannie are represented as masochistic victims, though the more harrowing characterisation is that of Lannie. Often likened by critics to Cassandra, she also speaks in the imagery of Keats; her references to a world of 'withered' grass in which 'no bird sings' (187) is that of 'La Belle Dame Sans Merci' – bleak, denatured, dead. This medieval allusion would be consistent with the Arthurian references throughout the novel. A blend of madness and acuity, in terms of the novel's putative allegory she stands for the smashed ideal of Trotsky's counterrevolution. No other character more painfully illustrates Mailer's vision of politics as a force for good or evil; in her unnatural bitterness and sudden angers, often self-directed, her voice is at times the most human we hear. Guinevere and Hollingsworth are to a degree natural partners, and there is even the feeling that in her Hollingsworth has found one of his kind – one of Lovett's last images is of Guinevere and Hollingsworth's voices together like 'the shrieking and caterwauling of animals washed over the dam' (307).

With Lannie – and Guinevere's daughter Monina – the picture is of innocence defiled. Lannie's 'story' is that of 'the princess who searched out evil for only that was left' (208), whose tragedy is that of the failed idealist who yet needs to believe in something, however masochistic – 'perhaps all that is left is to love the fire' (215). Both she and Guinevere submissively defer to Hollingsworth's dominance. Lovett hears Guinevere say to Hollingsworth, '"Oh, honey," she said in a weak tormented voice, "I'm confused. Will you tell me what to do? Will you always tell me what to do?"' (206), while Lannie says that Hollingsworth 'tells me what to do and then I do it, and so everything is simple now' (157). This last comes after one of the most disturbing passages in the novel, a stream-of-consciousness narrative, blasphemous and obscene, in which Lannie's sickness, like Hollingsworth's, is located in a context of sexual violence and debasement.

Mailer also attributes her self-hatred to a moral nature disfigured by the Holocaust. In what is the only extensive reference to the subject in his work as a whole, Lannie's guilt-stricken response is to see genocidal inhumanity as paradigmatic; Marxism proved to be a naïve and empty hope and now we must confront the hideous, depraved reality. She tells Lovett:

> It's only you who is the fool, and you will not recognize that all these years, ever since the great man sat on his piles in the British

Museum and let us think there was a world we could make, when all the time he was wrong, and we've been wrong, and there's no world to make for the world devours. . . . We never understood anything. There is a world, and this is what it is like: It is a tremendous prison, and sometimes the walls are opened and sometimes they are closed, but as time goes on they have to be closed more and more. Have you forgotten? Do you remember how the poorest of the poor used to be driven to the room where they were given death by gas? (212)

Barbary Shore is, finally, a novel of memorable parts, rather than a sustained artistic entity. Of its parts, Philip Bufithis is surely alone in his view that 'there is intensity of mood only in the last third of the novel when Lovett loses interest in his affair with Guinivere [sic] and befriends McLeod. The atmosphere changes from nervous stagnation to conspiratorial tension, and McLeod becomes the focus of the story'.[26] What Bufithis goes on to call McLeod's 'impassioned monologues'[27] have seemed to most of the novel's critics, indeed to Mailer also, the most egregious instance of the novel's loss of artistic control. Once McLeod takes to speechifying on the subjects of, *inter alia*, state capitalism versus monopoly capitalism, the economic imperative to war, and the inevitability of 'mankind in barbary' (282), he becomes the novel's saboteur. 'Towards the end the novel collapsed into a chapter of political speech and never quite recovered',[28] Mailer was forced to admit. Yet what he attempted in the novel as a whole was an explicitly political fiction, a type not at all common in the American literary tradition, nor to the novel in English generally. Without models upon which to build, and in the midst of a period of radical change in both life and ideology, Mailer later realised he had been 'trying for something which was at the very end of my reach, and then beyond it'.[29] He would never again use the novel as a vehicle for political expression in such an overt manner, though he would go on to become a political journalist of the highest calibre.

* * *

If in *Barbary Shore* the American slide into moral darkness was set primarily in a rooming house with all its connotations of disconnected and alienated lives, four years later in his next novel, *The Deer Park*, Mailer would again choose a setting to emphasise the frightening emptiness of American society, this time at the opposite end of the social scale. The novel is set in Desert D'Or, a version of Palm Springs, 'a pleasure resort where the movie great come to rest and disport themselves' as the first edition dustjacket says.[30] In this novel, as in both his previous books, the America on view is circumscribed, contained within the microcosmic community of Desert D'Or. In N*aked* 'The Time Machine' represents fragmentary capsules of American experience, and in *Barbary Shore* we have a society of interiors. Now, in his third novel, he offers us another enclave, this time one linked in decadence to the court of King Louis XV. The novel's epigraph, from Mouffle D'Angerville's *Vie Privée de Louis XV*, describes Louis's carnal playground:

> ... the Deer Park, that gorge of innocence and virtue in which were engulfed so many victims who when they returned to society brought with them depravity, debauchery and all the vices they naturally acquired from the infamous officials of such a place.

The first chapter, though noticeably informed by the narrative rhythms of Scott Fitzgerald, a debt Mailer later fully acknowledged,[31] is one of the most memorable in his fiction. *The Deer Park* recalls Fitzgerald's Hollywood novel *The Last Tycoon* only in relatively minor ways,[32] but in Mailer's inspired opening, with its vision of Desert D'Or as a Californian designer-Hell, he inscribes another circle to that abode of the damned in *The Great Gatsby*, the Valley of Ashes. As critic Max F. Schulz puts it,

> Desert D'Or burns without surcease from a sulfurous sky that blasts every living thing and from the lusts of the flesh that enthrall every inhabitant ... like those living in the Valley of

Ashes the sojourners of this desert community are indistinguishable in appearance and spirit from the landscape.[33]

However, unlike Fitzgerald's ash heaps of 'already decomposing . . . ash gray men', losers in the American push for material gain, Mailer's is a hell occupied by a special elect, a leisure-class living pointless lives, their talk 'made up of horses, stories of parties the night before, and systems for roulette' (4). Those who built Desert D'Or have effaced its history to produce a place where 'everything is in the present tense' (2). There is surely a Shelleyan echo in Mailer's reference to those chasing fool's gold, now lost to time like the once-mighty works of Ozymandias:

> Built since the Second World War, it is the only place I know which is all new. A long time ago, Desert D'Or was called Desert Door by the prospectors who put up their shanties at the edge of the oasis and went into the mountains above the desert to look for gold. But there is nothing left of those men; when the site of Desert D'Or was chosen, none of the old shacks remained. (1–2)

Shelley's poem 'Ozymandias' (the Greek name for King Rameses II, whose dynasty would be part of Mailer's subject nearly thirty years later in his sixth novel, *Ancient Evenings*) is a sonnet on human vanity and its monuments, now crumbling in the desert sands –

> Nothing beside remains. Round the decay
> Of that colossal wreck, boundless and bare
> The lone and level sands stretch far away.[34]

Architectural folly is very much a part of Mailer's subject in this opening chapter. For the first time in his work he displays a willingness to see American architecture and design as a key part of his cultural criticism. In his later culture-readings, particularly those published in *The Presidential Papers* (1963) and *Cannibals and Christians* (1967), he would condemn the 'totalitarian' design of urban America like some latter-day Ruskin. 'Mafia architects with their Mussolini Modern' are blighting the continent with their 'landscapes of psychosis':

> The totalitarian impulse not only washes away distinctions but looks for a style in buildings ... which will diminish one's sense of function and reduce one's sense of reality by reducing such emotions as awe, dread, beauty, pity, terror, calm, horror, and harmony.[35]

In Desert D'Or the architecture is already that 'empty promiscuous panorama'[36] Mailer would castigate in *Cannibals and Christians*. Repeatedly in his essays on the postwar architectural scene he draws attention to its sterility and emptiness, its contempt for tradition and the past all seen as external signs of that voiding of the spirit central to his definition of totalitarianism. 'The landscape of modern man takes on a sense of endless empty communications', he wrote in a 1965 essay for *The New York Times Magazine*, the walls of America's 'blank skyscrapers ... dead as an empty television screen'.[37] Later in his career Mailer would describe himself as a 'left conservative', and in his animadversions on the subject of contemporary architecture his radical conservatism is manifest. Writing on the subject in 1972, Richard Poirier even went so far as to argue that this cultural conservatism with 'its unmodified opposition to technology and its confidence in the possibility of small communities or neighbourhoods united organically by shared values, smacks always of agrarianism'.[38] Certainly Mailer can sound nostalgic and somewhat tendentious in his assessments of declining contemporary standards. His previews of a New York uprooting its architectural heritage, its brownstone buildings 'replaced by a cube sixteen stories high with a huge park for parking cars and a little grass', and his unfavourable comparisons between an ugly and denatured present full of 'industrial sludge' and the organic society of 'old neighbourhoods ... where the tradition of the nineteenth century and the muse of the eighteenth century still linger on the mood in the summer cool of an evening', are typical of the Mailer outlook.[39]

He shares much here with Robert Lowell, one of the most politically committed American poets of the postwar years and, with Mailer, an activist on the political front against the Vietnam War in the 1960s. The two men linked arms in October 1967, leading participants in the extraordinary citizen-army that marched on the Pentagon to protest the war, and in his great poem 'For the Union Dead' (1956), Lowell charts the nation's moral collapse in a structure that compares a Bostonian landscape of contemporary squalor with nineteenth-century old glory. Revisiting childhood haunts, Lowell's speaker finds only 'broken windows' and a city without respect for its past, uprooting it and cementing it over. The tone is best described by Mailer, who might well have had the poem in mind when he wrote:

> some part of us is aware that to uproot the past too completely is a danger beyond measure. It must at the least produce a profound psychic discomfort. . . . To return to an old neighborhood and discover it has disappeared is a minor woe for some; it is close to a psychological catastrophe for others, an amputation where the lost nerves still feel pain.[40]

The poem is suffused with the imagery of loss, and of outrage:

> I often sigh still
> for the dark downward and vegetating kingdom
> of the fish and reptile. One morning last March,
> I pressed against the new barbed and galvanised
> fence on the Boston Common. Behind their cage,
> yellow dinosaur steamshovels were grunting
> as they cropped up tons of mush and grass
> to gouge their underworld garage.
>
> Parking spaces luxuriate like civic
> sandpiles in the heart of Boston.[41]

Here is the 'huge car park', the 'industrial sludge' and the uprootedness of Mailer's hideous city, one that many of us may feel we have got to know all too well in the years since Lowell and Mailer wrote.

In Desert D'Or we have an early blueprint for this architecture of nightmare. In the first place it is 'all new', all signs of its past eradicated. It kills the concept of neighbourhood by being overwhelmingly a city of walls; it is denatured, arid, 'a place where no trees bear leaves' and the only grass to be found is the well-tended set of lawn-tennis courts at the Yacht Club, the resort's most exclusive hotel. Mailer's narrator, Sergius O'Shaugnessy, lives in a typical residence:

> I could describe the house in detail, but what would be the use? It was like most of the houses in the resort; it was modern, ranch-style, of course . . . and it had a garden and a wall which went around the garden, the standard fault of Desert D'Or architecture; along the desert table, the walls were made of glass to have a view of mesa-colored sand and violet mountains, but the houses were so close to each other that the builders had to fence them in, and the result was like living in a room whose walls are mirrors. In fact, my house had a twenty foot mirror which faced the wall of plate-glass window. No matter where I stood in the living room, I could never miss the sight of my rented garden with its desert flowers and the lone yucca tree. (3)

As Donald L. Kaufmann notes, 'narcissism shapes all interior decoration'[42] in Desert D'Or, and though it would be another decade before Mailer would develop the concept, its buildings clearly exemplify that 'totalitarian impulse [which] washes away distinctions', writ large in his vision of the mid-1960s.

'*The Deer Park* is a small, sour book with flashes of macabre wit',[43] wrote George Steiner in his review of the novel, and his reference to its 'macabre wit' is certainly an allusion to the character of Marion Faye who, like Cummings, Croft and Hollingsworth is yet another instance of what Poirier called 'the truth that perversity and power' were what interested Mailer as subjects,[44] a view shared apparently by Marilyn Monroe, who after reading *The Deer Park* told W. S. Weatherby that Mailer was 'too impressed by power'.[45] Critics have been divided as to which of the three candidates – Sergius O'Shaugnessy, Charles Eitel or Marion Faye – can best be described as the novel's 'hero'. Once again Mailer chose a first-person narrator, once again he introduces himself as an orphan, again he bears the scars of war, both psychic and physical (this time made impotent), and yet again he emerges as a curiously attenuated figure who comes to Desert D'Or, as Lovett to the Brooklyn rooming-house, adrift on the postwar currents, without much idea of a future except that, again like Lovett, he has a wish to become a novelist. For a great deal of his narrative, O'Shaugnessy is exactly that and little more, a narrator. If it was Mailer's intention to emulate Scott Fitzgerald's success in *The Great Gatsby*, where the narrator Nick Carraway is also firmly situated within the plot dynamic (in the 'Fourth Advertisement for Myself' Mailer referred to O'Shaugnessy's style as one which 'at its best sounded like Nick Carraway in *The Great Gatsby*'[46]), he failed in the effort. As Richard Foster noted, 'both as character and as an archetype of new styles of human value, [O'Shaugnessy] is vague and inchoate as well as faintly absurd . . . he is not very much more fully realized as an exemplar of new values in action than was his predecessor, Lovett'.[47] Marvin Mudrick simply dismisses O'Shaugnessy as 'a grand lacuna into which whole chapters topple and vanish'.[48] In the novel's second half it is true that O'Shaugnessy is rather absent, as Mailer shifts attention to the love affair between Charles Eitel and Elena Esposito. As Kaufman summarises, at that point O'Shaugnessy's 'point-of-view becomes that of a mere first-person observer with omniscient powers'. Later, 'after settling in New York, O'Shaugnessy becomes a sort of visionary observer . . . then follows a final chapter where the narrator sees into the future'.[49] Such narrative diversity could only have been successful had O'Shaugnessy been, like Nick Carraway, a character of sufficient strength in his own right. Unfortunately this is not the case. Mudrick is being only slightly too harsh in describing O'Shaugnessy as 'a stick'.[50]

Reviewing the novel for The *New Yorker* Brendan Gill described O'Shaugnessy as 'a young man with a preposterous name . . . and a scarcely less preposterous history, which he hurls at us in anguished gobbets'.[51] When O'Shaugnessy begins to confess his psychic ills we are not impressed by their rendition, wincing in the presence of the sort of writing – contrived, perfunctory, dull – that is completely absent from *The Naked and the Dead* though more present in *Barbary Shore*. And to argue that the real story in the novel is that of Eitel and Esposito, and not primarily that of O'Shaugnessy, is to miss the fundamental point that an involved first-person narrator must have some credibility of his own – the narrative lives, after all, in his consciousness.[52] To take *The Great Gatsby* as the model again (the comparison with Fitzgerald's masterpiece is perhaps unfair, though *The Deer Park* was Mailer's third novel as *Gatsby* was Fitzgerald's; also critics have compared Mailer's effort favourably with Fitzgerald's), Fitzgerald gives Carraway an opportunity to establish himself in a number of crucial ways before introducing readers to Gatsby and his milieu. As a moral force, as a poetic sensibility, as one interested in his *own* youth and its story as much as Gatsby's – in these senses and others Fitzgerald substantiates Carraway's presence as much more than a mere narrative device. He becomes our anchor, our guide. As a result we do not question his Olympian survey at the end, knowing that its validity, its gravity has been earned by the older Carraway of the novel's opening – wise, sad, salted by the years since Gatsby's death. In *The Deer Park* though, Mailer is too anxious to have his narrator tell of lives other than his own:

> I do not know if I can explain that I did not want to feel too much, and I did not want to think. I had the idea that there were two worlds. There was a real world as I called it, a world of wars and boxing clubs and children's homes on back streets, and this real world was a world where orphans burned orphans. It was better not even to think of this. I liked

the imaginary world in which almost everybody lived. The imaginary world. But I write too much. . . . Before the movie colony had been in Desert D'Or a week, what little story I have to tell was fairly begun. (47)

Better not to feel, to think, or to write too much about 'the real world', which is of course that of his own experience – if Mailer had only allowed O'Shaugnessy to develop as a character, we might have had fewer 'gobbets' and a more credible anguish.

The 'little story' O'Shaugnessy tells is of his relationships with Hollywood's beautiful and damned: Charles Francis Eitel (the surname to be pronounced eye-TELL as a not very subtle means of denoting his role as a Hollywood director who co-operated with the House Un-American Activities Committee and its Communist purge in the late 1940s); his mistress Ellen Esposito (regarded by most critics as Mailer's most convincing female character); Lulu Meyers, a sub-Monroe movie siren who is Eitel's ex-wife; Howard Teppis, a caricature of a Hollywood studio boss; and, most memorably, Marion Faye, the one character who seems an authentic, if odious, creation. This is the core group, but beyond them, as Brendan Gill remarked, we have the sense that 'Desert D'Or consists almost entirely of shrewd, gross, hard-drinking and sexually exacerbated swine'.[53]

As many critics have seen, with *The Deer Park* Mailer moves away from the ideological orientation of his previous work towards a new imperative of self. Thus Nigel Leigh tells us that 'for the first time in Mailer's fiction Marxism fails to function as an epistemology which makes the world more intelligible . . . what replaces ideology is an absorption with the individual'.[54] This new tendency is most clearly seen in the relationship between Eitel and O'Shaugnessy. At the start of his narrative the latter confesses to having 'always felt like a spy or a fake' (21), and in Eitel he finds a model of integrity, honesty and humanity who yet fails to sustain these values, in the end bequeathing them to O'Shaugnessy himself (yet another resemblance between this novel and *Barbary Shore*, which concludes with McLeod bequeathing the 'little object' to Lovett). As a result O'Shaugnessy is able to turn his back on Desert D'Or and his unsatisfactory affair with Lulu Meyers, and to begin living authentically. According to Frank McConnell, Sergius's 'imagination is inflamed, liberated, made fruitful by the spectacle of his great friend's ruin'.[55] He learns the first of Mailer's existential commandments — 'that law of life so cruel and so just which demanded that one must grow or else pay more for remaining the same' (346). He has learned this from Eitel who knows that 'the essence of spirit . . . was to choose the thing which did not better one's position but made it more perilous' (257).[56] Eitel himself fails to abide by that cruel commandment, though it would resurface in Mailer's work to become the most axiomatic element informing that new heroism of hip as defined in 'The White Negro'. O'Connell argues that 'the plot of *The Deer Park* is largely the plot of Sergius's deliverance from that uncomfortable feeling of being "a spy or a fake"'.[57] Eitel is the agent of this deliverance; his last words to O'Shaugnessy being 'I've always been as honest with you as I could . . . you're old enough now to do without heroes' (308). Though he fails to live up to his own standards in three main ways (for Stanley Gutman, who sees that Eitel 'surrenders his integrity and principles by making a deal with the Norton [HUAC] Committee . . . he fails his art, sacrificing his vision for the power that he gains by creating tasteless and mediocre products . . . and finally Eitel fails in love'[58]), he is yet the most warmly human of all Mailer's early heroes. Gutman argues that Eitel is in the mould of such predecessors as Hearn and McLeod —' he represents, for Mailer, the failure of the liberal spirit in the era of post-industrial, capitalist society'.[59] Yet he is, much more than McLeod and Hearn, a charismatic figure, and unlike them he has the artist's conscience, or has once had it:

> 'For you see', he confessed in his mind, 'I have lost the final desire of the artist, the desire which tells us that when all else is lost . . . there still remains that world we may create, more real to us, more real to others, than the mummery of what happens, passes, and is gone. So, do try Sergius', he thought,

'try for that other world, the real world, where orphans burn orphans and nothing is more difficult to discover than a simple fact. And with the pride of the artist, you must blow against the walls of every power that exists, the small trumpet of your defiance.' (374)

Yet though Mailer seems to give Eitel the last restorative word in O'Shaugnessy's rehabilitation, it is not Eitel, but Marion Faye who emerges as the most significant figure in *The Deer Park*. Variously described as a 'moral insurrectionary',[60] 'a truly brilliant portrait of a pimp-homo-hetero-satanic figure',[61] and 'an apocalyptic Tiresias' who is 'unquestionably the most intriguing character'[62] in the novel, it is Faye who dominates the novel's philosophical centre. If Desert D'Or is a deer park for debauchees, Faye is its doyen. As I noted in my introductory chapter, the novel was turned down by seven publishers on grounds of obscenity before finally being accepted by Putnam's. The offending passage amounted to what Mailer called 'six not very explicit lines about the sex of an old producer [Teppis] and a call girl'.[63] As the lines were published it is clear that an act of fellatio takes place, but with this scene alone it would be difficult to argue, as Laura Adams does, that 'the book's real accomplishment ... was to push back the frontier of sex in the serious novel'.[64] Robert Merrill defends Mailer from the charge of obscenity, thinking it 'strange that a writer who hates pornography as much as Mailer does should be plagued by the accusation that his own works are obscene'.[65] Harold Bloom also regards Mailer as 'a passionate and heterodox moralist',[66] and certainly those readers expecting to find *The Deer Park* pornographically bold would be disappointed. Mailer may well have raised salacious expectations with his epigraph from D'Angerville, and merely by populating Desert D'Or with a Hollywood *demimonde* he was inevitably associating the book with that popular mythology which proposed that the movie capital 'holds the keys to the ultimate arcanum of sex'.[67] Nigel Leigh is quite correct in his conclusion that 'the novel's reputation as sexually advanced is ... unwarranted', having more to do with what he calls 'Mailer's cunning promotion of the repressive actions of Putnam and Rinehart'.[68] If the censors were worried that the novel would deprave its readership, they ought perhaps to have looked more closely at the character of Marion Faye.

There is a clear connection between salient aspects of Faye's personality and Mailer's later delineation of the Hipster and the heroes of his next two novels, *An American Dream* and *Why Are We in Vietnam?* Many critics have drawn attention to this, but few have stressed that the dominant aspects of his mentality are deeply pernicious and inhuman. His misanthropy and self-hatred lead him towards what Diana Trilling calls 'an acute intimacy with the criminal and the psychopath in himself'.[69] He despises human weakness, seeing it every day in those who use his services as the colony's pimp. The novel's thirteenth chapter is an extraordinary portrait of his inhumanity, scored much more deeply than anything to be found in either Cummings or Hollingsworth, since Faye's is a determined embrace of inhumanity. He has an inflamed insight into his own pathology. 'Life was a battle against sentiment' (155) he believes, and sets about eradicating any residual trace of love or compassion in himself. Ironically he is the one character who absolutely condemns the sexual impulse, regarding it as a species of craven enslavement – 'he could be impregnable if sex was of disinterest to him and that was how to be superior to everybody else. That was the secret to life. It was all upside down, and you had to turn life on its head to see it straight' (156).

For the Hipster, the sexual act is the supreme statement of being, and, even more so, of becoming, an inexhaustible movement towards essence, 'the unachievable whisper of mystery within the sex, the paradise of limitless energy and perception just beyond the next wave of the next orgasm'.[70] For Faye, however, as for Hollingsworth, the movement is not towards mystical consummation, but towards sadism and brutality; he tells O'Shaugnessy,

> 'You find a hundred chicks, you find two hundred. It gets worse than dull. It makes you sick. I swear you start thinking

of using a razor. I mean, that's it,' he said, waving a finger like a pendulum, 'screwing the one side, pain the other. Killing. The whole world is bullshit.' (17)

It needs to be seen, then, that if *The Deer Park* is a novel concerned with obscenity (rather than 'an obscene novel') most of the obscenity is to be found in Marion Faye's evil mentality. Not all critics, unfortunately, have made this discrimination. Leigh is right to argue that 'Faye has radically broken down his own sexuality, perversely contributing to the decadence he abominates',[71] but Diana Trilling, in what is a crucial misjudgement, regards Faye not as the fascist psychopath he is but goes so far as to present him as a saviour:

> Faye is not God the Father, but he is in training to be God the Son. Dying for us, the Hipster becomes our savior; he is the resurrection and the life in a society of call girls who, will-lessly submitting to their poor destinies, can promise us nothing but further desperation and enervation.[72]

Most of the lives we see in Desert D'Or are for the most part failed and futile, but many still demand the compassion that Faye cruelly, and with relish, denies them. As the most 'infamous official' in the deer park, this 'savior' of the world prays in the end for its destruction:

> So let it come, Faye thought, let this explosion come, and then another, and all the others, until the Sun God burned the earth. Let it come, he thought, looking into the east at Mecca where the bombs ticked while he stood on a tiny rise of ground trying to see one hundred, two hundred, three hundred miles across the desert. Let it come, Faye begged, like a man praying for rain, let it come and clear the rot and the stench and the stink, let it come for all of everywhere, just so it comes and the world stands clear in the white dead dawn. (161)

4
A Plunge into the Age: *An American Dream* and *Why Are We in Vietnam?*

Mailer would wait a full decade before writing his next novel, *An American Dream*, in 1965. It was published in slightly revised book form in March of that year, after having appeared in the magazine *Esquire* in eight monthly instalments commencing January 1964. Though financially motivated,[1] Mailer soon found that writing under such pressures had unexpected compositional advantages:

> Writing the serial is in itself fun. It makes me work. Since it's been eight years since I've set out to write a novel and finish it, I think I would have taken forever to get somewhere if it weren't for the fact that I have to make my decisions in great haste and stick by them . . . you have to take the bold choice each time, because you know you can depend on getting something out of the bold effects – the subtler choices may prove to be too subtle and fail to come to life in the speed with which you have to write.[2]

To read *An American Dream* after *The Deer Park* is to experience all of the delights of a writer in confident possession of a new style, one which would serve Mailer well throughout the 1960s. This style – energetic, full of connections, restless – had been forming itself in his non-fiction, in *Advertisements for Myself* and *The Presidential Papers*, both of which had appeared as the decade opened, in 1959 and 1963 respectively. Mailer developed this style to good effect in *An American Dream*, where his first-person hero, Steve Rojack, is established from the start as a very strong presence in the narrative. Where both Lovett and O'Shaugnessy were often little more than narrative devices tending towards self-effacement, in *An American Dream* we are quickly provided with a cognitive map of Rojack's mind. The novel's opening chapter has a good deal to say about the formation of that mind – the traumas of war, the public life, the society marriage which Rojack will shortly terminate by strangling his wife to death. Above all though, Rojack's is the voice to express Mailer's 'bold effects', the voice of an American for whom the American Dream of power, fame, riches, has no further meaning.

By the mid-1960's Mailer had become one of the most dominant voices of the decade. According to literary historian Alfred Kazin, Mailer's fiction of the 1960s is memorable because his 'fantasies and ideas broke into the texture of every fiction he now wrote . . . Mailer succeeded in imposing his personal sense of things, as he did not his novels'.[3] Although Kazin offers this as a way of stressing the impact Mailer had upon the liberal imagination in America at that time, it also seems to imply a failure to find a successful correlative for this in fiction. Yet it seems to me that with *An American Dream* Mailer was able to control the vision and the voice in precisely the ways that both his two previous novels could muster only fitfully. Moreover, in *An American Dream*, he exploits his celebrity, or rather the celebrity of his ideas, in a way never previously available to the modern novelist. For the audiences of the mid-1960s – many of whom would have been familiar with the Mailer of *Advertisements*, the Mailer who consumed and was consumed by the new media-hunger, the Mailer who refused to be pigeonholed, his views aired in *Playboy* and *The New York Times* or in front of four thousand in Chicago where he debated with right-wing guru William F. Buckley Jr on the role of the right wing in American society – Mailer's ideas were a part of an emerging mass consciousness.

Coming upon Rojack's world in the pages of *Esquire* throughout 1964, many readers would already have been equipped with the necessary coordinates. In the years preceding the novel's publication, Mailer had first consolidated and then manipulated his reception by the mass media in order to convey what Kazin called 'his personal sense of things'. He vigorously exploited the cultural revolution of the period which saw old-time divisions of high brow and low brow begin to disintegrate. When *An American Dream* was released into this climate it became a text of potent and manifold appeal. By serialising the novel in *Esquire*, Mailer had ensured that it would become an ongoing 'event' in the mass marketplace over a span of months. After continuing exposure in a national magazine, the novel when eventually published immediately sold 50,000 copies and put Mailer back in the best-seller lists for the first time since *The Naked and the Dead*. If, then, his 'fantasies and ideas broke into the texture of every fiction he now wrote', this was very much a part of his strategy leading towards his stated goal of 'making a revolution in the consciousness of our time'.[4]

Although Mailer's new style was one of the most distinctive aspects of *An American Dream*, it is difficult to avoid the sense that appraisals which focus on style to the relative neglect of the novel's subject-matter are dodging the most notorious issue associated with it. Certainly the stylistic virtuosity of the novel was not considered by those reviewers who led the moral outcry against it. For however impressive Mailer's craftsmanship, this novel, which concludes with its hero an unpunished fugitive murderer, and its many images of violence and sexual perversion, was more than any other of his books responsible for the perception of him as a gravely irresponsible public figure. Pauline Kael lamented the paradox of Mailer as America's 'greatest writer . . . [since] what is unfortunate is our greatest writer should be a bum'.[5] For Jean Radford the criticism is similar, that 'behind the brilliant and elaborate surface of the language, Rojack and his author's attitudes appear to me to be bigoted, histrionic and reactionary'.[6] On publication the novel was most famously condemned by Elizabeth Hardwick, who in the pages of Philip Rahv's anti-Mailer *Partisan Review* described the novel as:

> A fantasy of vengeful murder, callous copulations and an assortment of dull cruelties. It is an intellectual and literary disaster, poorly written, morally foolish and intellectually empty.... *An American Dream* is a very dirty book – dirty and extremely ugly ... the environment [of the book] is made up of a crippling wife-hatred, degrading sexual boasting.... Mailer has not been able to transform Rojack or his murder. They come to us without art and without inspiration.[7]

Marvin Mudrick turned outrage to ridicule in describing the book as one which 'reads like Frank Sinatra's memoirs ghostwritten by Anaïs Nin. It is so absolute a fiasco that one hopes, without confidence, that it was done only for money'.[8] More recently, Martin Amis reminded us that 'in the Evelyn Waugh *Letters* Mailer is briefly described as "an American pornographer". For this book, the description holds. It is the prose of a man in a transport, not of sexual excitement so much as the tizzy of false artistry.'[9]

Yet even at the time the novel had its admirers, those who were able to recognise its extraordinary contemporary relevance. For the morality of *An American Dream* is one that was a response to its historical moment. These points were noticed by the reviewer for *The New York Times Book Review*, who told his readers:

> In *An American Dream*, his first novel in 10 years, Norman Mailer burns his remaining bridges. He tells a sometimes bizarre, always violent, absolutely contemporary story of evil, death, and strange hope. Reading it is like flying an airplane with the instruments cross-wired. . . . Unwise, irresponsible, devoid of the charm that now passes for literature, it diagrams the pentacle around which so many of us dance with such fateful urgency.[10]

And Joan Didion too praised Mailer's insight into what she

called 'the essence of things'. Like Scott Fitzgerald, Mailer she argued was a chronicler; he too had 'that great social eye. It is not the eye for the brand name . . . it is rather some fascination with the heart of the structure, some deep feeling for the mysteries of power.'[11] It is unfortunate that much of the viciousness of the attack upon the novel, both in 1965 and since, has been of the *ad hominem* sort – Rojack for many was but another of Mailer's lurid self-advertisements, this time with a sly subtext; there were too many similarities between his own biography and Rojack's, the most conspicuous of them all being that both had inflicted grievous bodily injury upon their wives, in Deborah Kelly's case, injury of the terminal kind. If Rojack–Mailer thought he could get away with murder, and if Mailer believed he could use the novel as an elaborate apologia for his own knifing of former wife Adele Morales, then the judiciary of the New York literary establishment would expose and condemn him as the city's lawcourts had not. Adverse criticism of the novel has for the most part tended to represent it as reductively introspective: Rojack's metaphysics are idiosyncratic and facile, having relevance only to the cranky margins. Of those critics who do regard the novel as introspective, only Richard Poirier is able to see that introspection as defining a larger sensibility. Poirier credits Mailer and Robert Lowell with

> having created the *style* of contemporary introspection, at once violent, educated, and cool. Their language substantially extends the literary resources of English, and people will later turn to them in any effort to determine the shapes our consciousness has been taking'.[12]

So it is, I would argue, both necessary and credible to read *An American Dream* not primarily as a novel closed in on a singular identity, but rather as one that, perhaps more than any other of the 1960s, dramatised the national mood. Many critics have made passing reference to Rojack's allusion to John F. Kennedy in the novel's opening paragraph:

I met Jack Kennedy in November, 1946. We were both war heroes, and had just been elected to Congress. We went out one night on a double date and it turned out to be a fair evening for me. I seduced a girl who would have been bored by a diamond as big as the Ritz.[13]

Yet only one of Mailer's critics, Frank D. McConnell, has seen the crucial significance that Kennedy's assassination has for a true appraisal of Mailer's achievement in *An American Dream*. When one considers the immediate and traumatic impact the assassination had upon America's perception of itself, and when one also takes account of Mailer's well-known prior interest in Kennedy and his heroic potentialities, it is odd indeed that McConnell's insight is so exceptional. In a brief critique of the novel, McConnell wrote:

> If the assassination of Kennedy was, as it appears more and more to have been, the signal public disaster in the American imagination of the sixties, then no writer registered the force of its trauma more immediately or accurately than Mailer. It is surely not accidental that the year of the assassination saw Mailer's return to the novel [after a decade's hiatus], with the publication of *An American Dream* . . . a heavily ironic title, and one intimately related to the assassination and its aftermath – for the 'dream' is of violence, murder, vengeance, and rape. . . . *An American Dream*, in fact, takes the form of a mirror image of the Kennedy assassination. For if the nightmare forces of repressed violence were unleashed, against his will, against the radiantly successful Kennedy, Mailer gives us, in the fable of Rojack, a picture of an equally successful man's willing descent into the same spiritual maelstrom – which, implicitly, is the maelstrom beneath all our lives.[14]

Rojack is sometimes referred to as Mailer's version of the hero America looked for in Kennedy and never found, but McConnell's judgement is more accurate – Rojack's is a narrative reflecting the national discord and *agon* ensuing from the Dream smashed on 22 November 1963 in Dallas.

Mailer's next book, the anthology *Cannibals and Christians* (1967), is of importance for the above view of *An American Dream*. In the third paragraph of the very first piece, a report on his coverage of the Republican Party's 1964 convention, Mailer is already introducing Kennedy's death as having provoked national dysfunction:

> The country had never been the same since Kennedy was assassinated . . . some process of derailment, begun with Hemingway's death [Hemingway took his own life on 2 July 1961] and the death of Marilyn Monroe [6 August 1962], had been racing on now through the months, through the heavens . . . it would be easier to know that Oswald had done it all by himself, or as an accomplice to ten other men, or was innocent, or twice damned; anything was superior to that sense of the ship of state battering its way down swells of sea, while in the hold cargo was loose and ready to slide.[15]

And at precisely the mid-point in *Cannibals*, Mailer is even more explicit about the connections between *An American Dream* and the assassination of Kennedy, telling us that:

> less than eight weeks before the assassination, work was begun on *An American Dream*. The name of the formal villain in that novel comes up on the first page. It is Kelly – Barney *Oswald* Kelly. If psychic coincidences give pleasure to some I do not know if they give them to me.[16]

It is obvious that for Mailer his novel was to be seen as having had a profound, even uncanny connectedness to the tragic events in Dallas. Yet to my knowledge none of the novel's critics, not even McConnell, has explored the significances that such passages in *Cannibals* have for a proper estimation of Rojack's narrative. Far from being the 'intensely private novel'[17] of a writer caught up in a cul-de-sac of self-inflections, we need to situate it firmly within its context of cultural crisis; we need to see Rojack, his violence, supernaturalism and rejection of normative discourse as the first extraordinary response by an American writer to the national sickening. The novel is indeed an effort to 'diagram the pentacle', to confront and defend against the demonic forces which were felt with 'such fateful urgency' by many Americans.

Later in the same piece ('In the Red Light: A History of the Republican Convention in 1964'), Mailer returns to his conception of Kennedy as an American hero, a theme first celebrated in his essay of 1960, 'Superman Comes to the Supermarket'. Now, though, the emphasis is upon the cultural consequences of the hero's demise. National grief has taken a darkening turn into madness and psychic breakdown:

> Suddenly he was dead, and we were in grief. But then came a trial which was worse. . . . Now, we were going mad. It took more to make a nation go mad than any separate man, but we had taken miles too much. Certainties had shattered. Now the voice of our national nerves (our arts, our events) was in a new state. Morality had wed itself to surrealism . . . we had an art of the absurd; we had moral surrealism. Our best art was *Dr Strangelove* and *Naked Lunch*, *Catch-22*; *Candy* was our heroine; Jack Ruby our ageing juvenile; Andy Warhol, Rembrandt; our national love was a corpse in Arlington. . . . Yes, our country was fearful, half mad, inauthentic. It needed a purge.[18]

Rojack's was one of the first voices to sound the national nerves, *An American Dream* the first striking instance of a post-Kennedy moral surrealism in the American novel. Mailer's subsequent novel, *Why Are We in Vietnam?* (1967) is yet another extraordinary extension of this genre, a novel that defers explicit reference to the war until its minimal citation in the very last lines. Without the reference and the novel's title, it seems likely – given their predisposition to read *An American Dream* ahistorically – that reviewers and critics may well have overlooked the connection between the violent and obscene neuroses of Mailer's hunters and the obscene violence of America making war in south-east Asia. Mailer might even have had cause to regret the more open-ended title of the earlier novel (something like *An American Dream, or Life Without JFK* is devoid of subtlety, but so it seemed were most of Mailer's reviewers), which is, indeed, a distinct prelibation of his concerns in *Why Are We in Vietnam?* Rojack and his battles with the devils, warlocks, omens, wizards and fiends is a close relative of those new frontiersmen letting savage blood run free in the Alaskan Brooks Range. To read either novel ahistorically is to disregard Mailer's indisputable concern for the largest involutions of American history in the post war years.

In his speech at Berkeley on Vietnam Day in 1965, published in *Cannibals and Christians,* Mailer incorporated a slightly but significantly amended version of his comments on Kennedy cited above. The effect of the additional text is to find that the 'purge' needed to release all that backed-up and livid American ferment consequent upon Kennedy's murder, could only be accomplished by war:

> Our country was fearful, half-mad, inauthentic – it needed a war or it needed a purge. Bile was stirring in the pits of the national conscience. . . . We took formal steps toward a great society, that great society of computers and pills, of job aptitudes and bad architecture, of psychoanalysis, superhighways, astronauts . . . where censorship would disappear but every image would be manipulated from birth to death. Something in the buried animal of modern life grew bestial at the thought of this Great Society – the most advanced technological nation of the civilised world was the one now closest to blood, to shedding the blood and burning the flesh of Asian peasants it had never seen.[19]

National bloodlust is the issue of the totalitarian society Mailer had previewed as early as *The Naked and the Dead*. Now without Kennedy to symbolise and thereby partially contain the untapped potentialities (for he enfolded a mythology of romance,

A Plunge into the Age 93

of daring, of triumphalism – 'he won the biggest poker game we ever played' – facing down Khrushchev in the missile crisis of 1962[20]), Americans were like the cargo in the hold, loose and ready to slide, ready, like Rojack, to spill the blood of others. A quarter-century later, Mailer would find history repeating itself in the first years of the Bush presidency and would reiterate, almost word for word, the analysis cited above. In May 1991 in an article for *Vanity Fair* magazine, he saw contemporary American anguish 'sliding into the first real stages of fascism'.[21] Again social sickness, for which political medicine is unavailing, is endemic, though the underlying factors in the disease are many and finally inseparable – 'it did not matter whom your blamed':

> The fact was that America was mired in grievances, miseries, miscalculations, slave history, and obsessions; the economy was reflecting it. In fact, Mailer was surprised by something in himself. Something deep in him – which is to say, no longer censorable – was now saying: 'The country needs a purge, a fling, some sacrifice of blood, some waste of the blood of others, some colossal event, a triumph. We need an extravaganza to take us out of ourselves. We are Romans, finally, and there is no moral force left among our citizens to countermand that fact. So this war will be a crucial vacation from the morose state of American affairs. If it succeeds, the country may even be able to face a few real problems again.'[22]

As the country 'needed a war' in the aftermath of Kennedy's death, so Mailer writes after the Gulf War thirty years later, 'America needed to win a war.'[23] And during his visit to England in 1991 I asked him to further discuss his position on American involvement in the Gulf conflict. 'There was just so much phoniness and discontent and absolute rage in America', he told me, 'that we needed a war. We needed a war the way a marine needs a fight in a bar.'[24] The need for war, for a bloody purge, is attributed to America's moral bankruptcy, to its barbarism. 'Something in the buried animal of modern life' growing bestial at the thought of the Great Society in the 1960s has been answered by 'something deep' in Mailer, proposing himself as the representative American of the century's last decade. In Stephen Rojack we have the first personification of this impulse, of the American as Roman, of all the 'bile stirring in the pits' of the national life.

McConnell described *An American Dream* as a novel that 'takes the form of a mirror image of the Kennedy assassination', with Rojack as a case-study in the psychic consequences of that death. In his review of Victor Lasky's Kennedy biography, *JFK: The Man and the Myth*, a review written twelve weeks before the assassination, Mailer himself uses the mirror image, casting Kennedy as an American Narcissus:

> His magnetism is that he offers us a mirror of ourselves, he is an existential hero, his end is unknown, it is even unpredictable, even as our end is unpredictable, and so in this time of crisis he is able to perform the indispensable psychic act of a leader, he takes our national anxiety so long buried and releases it to the surface – where it belongs. Now we must live again as a frontier nation, out on a psychic frontier without the faith of children or the security of answers. So the country, for better or worse, is now again on the move, and the President is the living metaphor of our change. It is this power in him to excite – whether he desires it or not – our change, our discord, and our revolt, which [makes him] the agent of our ferment.[25]

These words are charged with a remarkable feel for the drama implicit in Kennedy's life, and in those references to his 'end' we have another instance of Mailer's sensitivity to future unfoldings, especially as he concluded the review by asking whether 'the final face of the Presidency and America shall prove to be Abraham Lincoln, [the assassinated sixteenth President] or Dorian Gray'.[26] Rojack's narrative is that of a killer whose Second World War experiences have left him death-haunted, 'lost in a private kaleidoscope of death' (15) as he puts it; as an academic – a professor of existential psychology – he believes that 'magic, dread, and the perception of death were the roots of motivation', and he is the author of what he calls 'one popular book . . . *The Psychology of the Hangman*, a psychological study of the styles of execution in different states and nations' (15). These predispositions may have seemed more topical than morbid to the readers of the novel's first serial instalment in January 1964, who may have agreed with Rojack that 'death is a creation more dangerous than life' (15).

In *An American Dream* we have then an extraordinary instance of the first American novel to have responded to the national trauma of late 1963. Rojack's emerging sociopathy finds its ultimate context in what Don DeLillo has called 'the seven seconds that broke the back of the American century'.[27] Kennedy is the backgrounded eminence who yet provokes buried energies to issue forth in violence. 'Jack Kennedy had a revolutionary effect on American life', wrote Mailer, 'and all variety of ferment grew out of his image.'[28] A very large part of the novel's participation in the resulting culture of 'moral surrealism' is Rojack's correspondence with the reality beneath appearances. Having murdered his wife he knows himself to be hunted but also haunted. 'Men were afraid of murder', he thinks, 'but not from a terror of justice so much as the knowledge that a killer attracted the attention of the gods' (206). He is tormented by all that is irrational; the New York night is alive to him with cries *de profundis* 'going out into an alley of the night, carrying across the miles to the thirty storeys of this room – was a murderer running and caught in the patrols of the gods?' (257). As a result of both giving death and understanding its ramifications for life, he can no longer believe 'that death was zero, death was everyone's emptiness' (15). His participation in public discourse ruptures:

> I had learned to speak in a world which believed in the *New York Times*: Experts Divided on Fluoridation, Diplomat Attacks Council Text, Self-rule Near for Bantu Province. Chancellor Outlines Purpose of Talks, New Drive for Health Care for Aged. I had lost my faith in all of that by now. . . . Yes, I had

come to believe in spirits and demons, in devils, warlocks, omens, wizards and fiends, in incubi and succubi. (43)

He has turned his back on a socio-political order which looks to political process and collective action as meaningful ways forward. This is the subtext of an America after Kennedy, whose death had unleashed 'the fearful, the half-mad', the absurdity of ever believing again in a language of reason and logic.

Don DeLillo's novel *Libra* (1988), one of the most memorable efforts to deal with all we have discovered, or not, about the assassination over the last twenty-five years, gives us multiple perspectives which orbit around the pivotal characterisation of Lee Harvey Oswald. One crucial perspective is that of Nicholas Branch, the chorus voice of *Libra*, a retired CIA senior analyst hired on contract to write 'the secret history' of the assassination for the Agency.[29] Yet for all his labour, the searches, siftings, studies of documents, files, 'the data-spew of hundreds of lives' connected, however tenuously, to the assassination, more than fifteen years of research leads Branch not to logical conclusions but rather to a mystical insight, to 'a strangeness, Branch feels, that is almost holy. There is much here that is holy, an aberration in the heartland of the real.'[30] This latter phrase precisely describes the epistemological crisis Rojack is experiencing throughout *An American Dream*. He becomes privy to an occult knowledge which is the retribution visited upon him as a murderer:

> For I wanted to escape from that intelligence . . . I wanted to be free of magic, the tongue of the Devil, the dread of the Lord, I wanted to be some sort of rational man again, nailed tight to details, promiscuous, reasonable, blind to the reach of the seas. But I could not move. (257)

Most critics of the novel who think well of it invariably read it as proposing the regeneration of its hero. For instance Laura Adams argues that Rojack is an American archetype who grapples with the Devil to emerge victorious 'with a sense of fresh possibility gained from this most elemental battle'. The novelist 'seems to be saying, America has long known how to murder, let her now learn how to create. . . . Mailer offers an imaginative possibility for the future.'[31] And Max F. Schulz contends that the novel's ethic is progressive, from vice to virtue – 'in the course of twenty-four hours Rojack progresses from lust to love, from sodomy to fruitful coition, from selfish wilfulness to willed self-lessness . . . from the neighbourhood of hell to the environs of heaven'.[32] Yet though it is true that Rojack does, very fleetingly, find his moment of tender love with Cherry, the fact remains that he is unable to brave the trials of a Harlem night in order to save her life and their love (for according to his metaphysic, 'God was not love but courage. Love came only as a reward – 206). Their union is no blissful climacteric but is attenuated on all sides by the beating and death of Cherry's ex-lover Shago Martin, the failed propitiation of Rojack's walk back along Barney Kelly's parapet which is, in the narrative's occult schema, the failure of courage producing Cherry's death ('"The first trip was done for you," said the voice, "but the second was for Cherry," and I had a view of the parapet again and the rain going to ice, and was afraid to go back' – 263), and most conspicuously by the novel's epilogue, in which death and madness are integral to Rojack's atmosphere, inside and out.

In the epilogue we see that what McConnell calls 'the fable of Rojack' leads not to paradise and redemption as some would have it,[33] but rather to an increasingly maddened and death-engulfed milieu. His murder of wife Deborah may go 'unpunished' in legally retributive terms (reviewers Philip Rahv and Elizabeth Hardwick both condemned the novel's morality on such grounds), but Rojack pays for the act in other ways. As Joseph Wenke puts it, 'the novel does dramatise a form of divine retribution, for in committing murder, Rojack has attracted the attention of the gods, exposing himself to an invasion of magical forces that is finally overwhelming'.[34] The turn towards death in American society is clearly a major element in this novel's vision. As Poirier suggested, the novel's treatment of the sexual act 're-veals Mailer's increased revulsion from all kinds of sexuality that are, in the literal sense of the word, degenerate, that express what he takes to be the de-creative impulse' in American society.[35] And the partnership between evil and power at the corrupt heart of the American establishment is forcefully conveyed in the penultimate chapter in the extraordinary exchanges between Kelly and Rojack. Such scenes are intended to illustrate the limitless reach of Kelly's power, a wholly evil being with the will, the means and the metaphysics to enforce the assassination of a President. 'I did not know where his power ended' (255) Rojack says to himself, but already he has sensed its byzantine grip upon the New York police, the Mafia and the CIA. In his presence, evil is palpable:

> The silence had no air left . . . and I slipped off the lip of all sanity into a pit of electronic sirens and musical lyrics dictated by X-ray machines for a gout of the stench which comes from devotion to the goat came up from him and went over to me. . . . Kelly was near to that violence Deborah used to give off, that hurricane rising from a swamp, that offer of carnage, of cannibals, the viscera of death came from him to me like suffocation. (256)

It *is* remarkable that the most egregious embodiment of evil in Mailer's fiction should, only weeks before Kennedy's death, have been named Oswald Kelly. Rojack is as unable to escape Kelly's signature, 'the viscera of death', as Americans to deny Lee Harvey Oswald his indelible signature upon their history. As DeLillo puts it in *Libra*, it was 'like a secret they'd keep forever . . . the true and lasting power of his name'.[36]

To escape that baleful stench of death, Rojack has to escape America. For America is the land of death according to the novel's epilogue, its characteristic odours those rising from the autopsy of a cancered body. Rojack encounters one such, courtesy of a doctor friend ('You write so much about death, Rojack, let this trooper show you some') on his drive towards Las Vegas, and its 'maniacal smell' pervades the continent:

A Plunge into the Age

I kept getting a whiff of the smell for the next two days, all along the trip through the dried hard-up lands of Oklahoma, northern Texas, New Mexico, on into the deserts of Arizona and southern Nevada where Las Vegas sits in the mirror of the moon. Then for weeks I never lost the smell. (267–8)

In Las Vegas he 'went into two atmospheres'; outside his hotel was 'the burned-out air, madnesses forming, madnesses consumed' (269), while inside was the air-conditioned nightmare, 'the second atmosphere [which] had a smell which was not the air conditioning of other places. . . . You caught the odour of an empty space where something was dying alone' (270). Our final vignette of Rojack's American city is of 'a new breed of man', living in this second atmosphere 'for twenty-three hours of the twenty-four', hiding, dying in its empty cold spaces, and our final glimpse of Rojack before he flees America for 'Guatemala and Yucatan' is of his conversation with the dead:

I wandered on, and found a booth by the side of the empty road, a telephone booth with a rusty dial. Went in and rang up and asked to speak to Cherry. And in the moonlight, a voice came back, a lovely voice, and said, 'Why, hello, hon, I thought you'd never call. It's kind of cool right now, and the girls are swell. Marilyn says to say hello. We get along, which is odd, you know, because girls don't swing.' (271)

For Leslie Fiedler 'it is a long way from the beginning of Mailer's book to the end: from his evocation of the dead Dream Boy of us all [Kennedy] . . . to the Dead Dream Girl of us all [Monroe]'.[37] Yet the distance between them is not nearly so great as the distance separating them both from that postlapsarian graveyard of American dreams which Kennedy's death foretold. It was a bell which tolled the end of the spirit of liberal idealism in America and, as Mailer wrote in 1992 (reviewing Oliver Stone's film *JFK*), 'no afternoon in the recollection of our lives is equal to November 22, 1963, and in its aftermath we lost our innocence'.[38] It is, surely, significant that *An American Dream* remains the firs only two novels (the other being *Ancient Evenings*) that Mailer concluded with compositional dates. They are the text's final portent: 'Provincetown, New York, September 1963 – October 1964' (271).

By the end of his most prolific decade, Mailer would publish a further novel, *Why Are We in Vietnam?* (1967), and in addition to *Cannibals and Christians* (1966), a further six books.[39] Amongst the latter the most outstanding was *The Armies of the Night* (1968), a masterpiece of New Journalism which took both the National Book Award and the Pulitzer Prize in 1969 and, alone among his contemporaries, demonstrated Mailer's aptitudes as journalist, historian and mythographer, as the war in Vietnam became America's ideological civil war. His presence as the involved narrator of *Armies* expressed both the cultural analyst as well as the political activist in him. The book's title, taken from Matthew Arnold's mid-Victorian poem 'Dover Beach' ('And we are here as on a darkling plain / Swept with confused alarms of struggle and flight, / Where ignorant armies clash by night'),[40] suggests much that links the 1960s with the 1860s, but also implies Mailer's title to the vacant position of commanding officer. Perhaps he regretted the cancelled sortie which would have taken him to the Vietnam war-zone as a reporter for the *Herald Tribune* newspaper in 1966.[41] The paper faced financial collapse soon after and Mailer never visited Vietnam. Yet the author of *The Naked and the Dead* discovered a new battleground emerging upon the streets of Chicago and the steps of the Pentagon.

Both *Armies* and *Why Are We in Vietnam?* are works that show the profundity with which Mailer in both imagination and in fact was engaged with the causes and the consequences of Vietnam. When most of his American writing peers were all but voiceless, unable or unwilling to assess the effects of war upon American culture (for instance, Saul Bellow's novel of the war's middle years, *Mr Sammler's Planet* – 1969 – contains not a single reference to Vietnam), *Why Are We in Vietnam?* provided what Philip

A Plunge into the Age

Beidler has recently referred to as a work of 'mythic resourcefulness [which] creates an "experience" of Vietnam as true as any that ever existed in fact'.[42] Throughout the 1980s American responses to the defeat in Vietnam were conspicuous – in a revisionist historiography of the war, in popular culture's trivialisation in such forms as the *Rambo* cycle of Hollywood films, and more recently in the Gulf War which President Bush took as a victory over his nation's unhappy memories of the loss in Vietnam as much as over the ostensible foes. In 1967, however, only Mailer was able to offer America a studied image of its own madness. Taken together, *The Armies of the Night* and *Why Are We in Vietnam?* mark the climax to that vein of Mailer's thought commencing in *An American Dream* and sustained in *Cannibals and Christians*. Rojack's purge of violence is uncannily predictive of the national purge so awfully carried through in Indochina. With *Cannibals*, Mailer provided the analytical intertext which explained the mediations between Rojack and D.J., the latter a fully developed embodiment of that 'new breed of man' sketched in at the close of *An American Dream*.

Mailer wrote the novel in five months (May–September 1966) and it remains one of his briefest novels to date. Interviewed at the time of its publication, he spoke of its informing vision as one dealing with the psychotic American push to destroy Vietnam:

> I think a civilization is created out of some kind of sublimation of violence. When the violence gets too sublimated, you get a sick civilization. . . . What are we doing now? We're not only destroying a country, but we're literally destroying the foliage of that country. We're destroying God's work, not man's work but God's work. And at the same time we're pretending to be the deliverers of civilization. So I'd have to say we are psychotic.[43]

Certainly the majority of the novel's critics have acknowledged the extent to which in both style and subject-matter it exposes the sublimated neuroses responsible for the bellicose strain in 1960s America. For Joseph Wenke the novel is 'an experiment in excess, an attempt to imitate in prose the roaring madness of America',[44] while Frank McConnell argued that:

> The book is about Vietnam, so much so that one is led to wonder, in retrospect, if any other American writer could have imaged the real dimensions of that obscene adventure as fully as Mailer. Following immediately upon the national shame of the Kennedy assassination, the Vietnam war was, as much as any historical event could be, the bloody inhuman, divisive incarnation of that Great War of the Soul that Mailer's heroes ... had been prophesying about and preparing us for for nearly two decades.[45]

Because the novel suggested a more explicit psycho-political context than its predecessor, some recent critics have been more prepared to read his fiction of the 1960s as one characterised by allegory. So Stacey Olster, writing in 1989 could situate *An American Dream* in the same allegorical field as *Vietnam?*, giving it the larger context it was denied by most critics in the decade of its publication; she argues that 'because Mailer's purpose in each book is to show how American dreams can lead to nightmares like Vietnam, it is important to realize that the Alaskan landscape in *Vietnam?* is equivalent metaphorically to the sexual landscape in *An American Dream*'.[46]

The novel is set in the Alaskan wilderness, a setting about to be disturbed by the Texas huntsmen with their helicopters and techno-weaponry. As the wild animals are mutilated by this firepower, the narrative's allegorical coordinates seem straightforward. Indeed the dustwrapper blurb on the first British edition of the novel goes so far as to suggest this as one of two possible readings of it:

> Norman Mailer's new novel is about a hunting trip in Alaska. Vietnam, as it happens, is only mentioned once. Why then the title? Perhaps the question is answered obliquely by allegory! Or then again perhaps it can be read as a symbolic psychic ex-

planation of why America fights in Vietnam. The reader and the critic are left to draw their own conclusion.[47]

If the British publishers felt such meanings had to be spelled out due to American reviews (the novel was published a full two years earlier in America) which had questioned its relevance to the Vietnam war, later critics have been quite clear in seeing the Alaskan safari in allegorical terms. According to Laura Adams, Mailer uses 'hunted animals as a metaphor for the Vietnamese',[48] while for Joseph Wenke, 'the use of the helicopter turns the hunt into the moral equivalent of an unjust war'.[49] Philip Bufithis is also able to propose the same case, arguing that 'the hunting party is the American military in miniature',[50] and Robert Solotaroff finds an even more detailed political allegory, with two of the minor characters, Bill and Pete, 'playing Mc-Namara and Rusk to Rusty's LBJ'.[51]

The novel remains a nonpareil landmark of obscenity in the history of fiction written by major American novelists. Writing in *The Armies of the Night*, Mailer defended the obscenity of the language used in *Vietnam?* on two main counts. Firstly, by indulging what he termed the 'naturally obscene', he felt in touch with an authentic strain of the American vernacular. Returning to 'the happy play of obscenity upon concept' is like returning to that river running underground the hypocritical surface of American public life – 'the truth of the way it really felt over the years passed on a river of obscenity from small-town storyteller to storyteller there down below the bankers and the books and the educators and the legislators'.[52] Worse, those who were least naturally obscene, least connected to this river of creative obscenity, were most likely to accept the real obscenity of the war in Vietnam, 'perfectly capable of burning unseen women and children in the Vietnamese jungles'.[53] Obscenity is, here as elsewhere in Mailer's fiction (one thinks particularly of the connection between fascism and obscenity in Hollingsworth of *Barbary Shore*), an expression of depravity and inhumanity. But the narrating voices of *Why Are We in Vietnam?* show Mailer's willingness to discriminate between the creative obscenity of such voices, and the decreative mentality that is responsible for the obscenity of Vietnam. In an age which seemed incapable of making such discriminations, his use of obscenity became a vital political act, an effort to stimulate a moral vision in atrophied eyes:

> what was disappointing was the crankiness across the country. Where fusty old conservative critics had once defended the obscenity in *The Naked and the Dead*, they, or their sons, now condemned it in the new book, and that *was* disappointing.[54]

The novel's strengths have been stressed by critics in the years since, and particularly in recent times. Philip D. Beidler in his *Rereading Vietnam* (1992) regards the novel as one of the handful of classic accounts of the war years, seeing it alongside Michael Herr's *Dispatches* and William Eastlake's *The Bamboo Bed* as a work 'of indisputable genius',[55] while Ihab Hassan in 1990 wrote of it as 'possibly Mailer's best work', its prose 'astonishing, unique in American letters, the hip creation of a demiurge'.[56] Such assessments confirm Richard Poirier's much earlier judgement (1972) of it as 'perhaps his most brilliant and certainly one of his central texts'.[57]

There are at least two important sources for an understanding of Mailer's thought as it was developing in the years since *An American Dream* had appeared in book form in 1965. His most important essays on the subject of America and Vietnam in this period were collected in *Cannibals and Christians* (1966). Though some of these essays date from 1961–2, others are coterminous with his writing of *Why Are We in Vietnam?* In such essays as 'The Argument Reinvigorated', the introduction to Part Two of *Cannibals*, Vietnam is proposed as a further extension of that national pathology Mailer had identified seven years previously in the essay 'Superman Comes to the Supermarket': the national life still runs in two rivers, two versions of psychosis:

> Half of America went insane with head colds and medicaments and asthmas and allergies . . . and boredom, boredom

plague deep upon the land; and the other part of America went ape, and the motorcycles began to roar like lions across the land and all the beasts of all the buried history of America turned in their circuit and prepared to slink toward the market place, there to burn the mother's hair and bite the baby to the heart. One thought of America and one thought of aspirin, kitchen-commercials, and blood. One thought of Vietnam.[58]

This bleak vision of an America denatured, and with a broken-backed history had been integral to Mailer's view of his culture for at least the decade prior to 1967. With *Why Are We in Vietnam?* though, his thinking on the subject takes a new and even more despairing turn. His *Partisan Review* essay of 1965 concludes with an extraordinary three paragraphs which anticipate not only the vision and idiom of his own forthcoming novel, but also one of the major tropes informing such classic representations of the war as Francis Ford Coppola's film *Apocalypse Now* (1979). The idea of Vietnam as a theme park in which the young turks of America can have some real target practice in between surfing and being entertained by Playboy Bunnies airlifted in for a jungle *son et lumière* has, since *Apocalypse Now*, become a familiar one in Hollywood's Vietnam. Yet this notion of the war as a circus, the ultimate 'happening' of the tuned-in, turned-on 1960s, was anticipated in the final vision of Mailer's 'A Speech at Berkeley on Vietnam Day', one of his most famous public addresses and a landmark in the history of the anti-Vietnam war movement. In front of 20,000 people gathered to protest the war at the Berkeley campus of the University of California, Mailer gave a virtuoso performance, fastening at the close onto a satirical vision so memorably monstrous that it may have reached far beyond its immediate context:

> We're the greatest country ever lived for speeding up the time. So, let's do it right. Let's cease all serious war, kids. Let's leave Asia to the Asians. Let us, instead, have wars which are like happenings. Let us have them every summer. Let us buy a tract of land in the Amazon, two hundred million acres will

do, and throw in Marines and Seebees and Air Force ... invite them all, the Chinks and the Aussies, the Frogs and the Gooks and the Wogs, the Wops and the Russkies, the Yugos, the Israelis, the Hindoos, the Pakistanis. We'll have war games with real bullets and real flame throwers, real hot-wire correspondents on the spot, TV with phone-in audience participation, amateur war movie film contests for the soldiers, discotheques, Playboy Clubs, pictures of the corpses for pay TV, you know what I mean. ... Unless Vietnam is the happening. Could that really be? Little old Vietnam just a happening? Cause if it is, Daddy Warbucks, couldn't we have the happening just with the marines and skip all that indiscriminate roast tit and naked lunch, all those bombed-out civilian ovaries, Mr J., Mr L.B.J., Boss Man of Show Biz – I salute you in your White House Oval; I mean America will shoot all over the shithouse wall if this jazz goes on, Jim.[59]

Mailer himself returned to the notion three years later in *The Armies of the Night*, remarking that 'the most insane of wars was more sane than the most insane of games'.[60] But before that the motif of the war game had found its expression in the political allegory of *Why Are We in Vietnam?*, wherein Alaska is a rehearsal for the killing fields soon to be visited by two of the huntsmen, D.J. and Tex. Indeed, unmistakable in the above passage is the slangy idiom of that 'teen-age junkie', D.J., the involved narrator of the novel, who we are told takes 'the drug addict William Burroughs as his hero' (14). And Burroughs's vision of a madly disjunct America provides the second major source underwriting Mailer's thought in *Vietnam?* He had testified on behalf of Burroughs in the Boston obscenity trial of the latter's novel, *Naked Lunch*, in 1965, and in his *Partisan Review* essay of 1965 he suggested that in *Naked Lunch* Burroughs had epitomised the surrealistic hell of Vietnam, its literary correlative, for 'if World War II was like *Catch-22*, this war will be like *Naked Lunch*'.[61] As Solotaroff notes:

> the voice of *Naked Lunch*, which tells us that it is a writing in-

strument or a tape, profoundly anticipated the electronic yawp of Mailer's disc jockey in *Vietnam?*. . . the 'friendLee voice at your service' in the very first sentence of the novel reminds us that Lee is the name of one of Burroughs most important characters. In fact Burroughs first novel, *Junkie*, was published under the pseudonym of William Lee.[62]

What Mailer admired about *Naked Lunch* was its shocking vision of a future world in the grip of electronic nightmare. In his essay 'Some Children of the Goddess' (published in *Cannibals and Christians*), he celebrates the novel's ideas which 'have pushed into the frontier of an all-electronic universe':

> One holds onto a computer in some man-eating machine of the future which has learned to use language. The words come out in squeaks, spiced with static, sex coiled up with technology like a scream on the radar. Bombarded by his language, the sensation is like being in a room where three radios, two television sets, stereo hi-fi, a pornographic movie, and two automatic dishwashers are working at once while a mad scientist conducts the dials to squeeze out the maximum disturbance. If this is a true picture of the world to come, then Burroughs is a great writer.[63]

The voices in *Why Are We in Vietnam?* owe a good deal to that grotesquerie described above. Burroughs's novel was one of the first to conceptualise what now we would be sure to term the cultural phenomenon of postmodernism: a phenomenon in which surfaces refer to other surfaces, and the humanist ideal has been dissolved into a sensibility all too aware of the collapse of idealism. In the postmodern view, we are all finally nothing more than a crosshatch of discourses. In *Why Are We in Vietnam?* Mailer's ostensible narrator, D.J., represents this emerging sensibility, the product of a new post-Kennedy age of failed idealism; as John Aldridge has noted, it must be of more than passing significance that D.J. hails from Dallas, 'that Eden of assassinations'.[64] Mailer invests his narrator with that ironic self-consciousness so often found in the postmodern novel. At its most fundamental level, this irony includes the narrator's refusal to confirm his real identity. Instead he prefers to ask his readers (to whom he frequently refers using a range of insulting *sobriquets*) to believe his voice may be either that of an eighteen year old, the son of a wealthy Dallas family, or alternatively the voice of one who refers to himself as 'a Harlem Spade'. If we take the primary narrator to be the first of these alternatives, we have a narrative of memory as D. J. Jethroe recalls the Alaskan hunting trip he took two years previously with his father, Rusty, his friend Tex Hyde, and others. The whole narrative is being recollected in his doped-up head as he sits at a dinner table in the family home on the eve of his departure for Vietnam. Why does Mailer make the novel's point of view so problematic?

The novel's title suggests that Mailer's intention was to offer a dramatic analysis which would go far to explain the American presence in a conflict which had divided the nation. His choice of a first-person narrator who is himself about to become a combatant in the war was an obvious means of personifying the human origins and effects of that warlust which had led the nation into the disaster of Vietnam. The main problem with this narrative technique was that although it dramatised such a mentality well enough through the first-person view, it deprived us of a point of view which is detached from and critical of the war and the culture of violence upon which it is based. Without this detached witness (usually provided by a novelist's choice of a third-person narrator), Mailer would have had to employ a good deal of ironic context so as to undermine and discredit the likes of D.J. and his fellow hunters.[65] I would argue, however, that in the novel's final design Mailer avoids these problems by introducing an alternative narrator in the form of the 'Harlem Spade' and that, further, we should attribute the entire narration to Harlem rather than Dallas. In the novel's crucial final paragraph, it must be significant that Mailer finds it necessary to remind readers of the narrative possibilities:

tomorrow Tex and me, we're off to see the wizard in Vietnam.

A Plunge into the Age 109

Unless, that is, I'm a black-ass cripple Spade and sending from Harlem. You never know. You never know what vision has been humping you through the night. So, ass-head America contemplate your butt. Which D.J. white or black could possibly be worse of a genius if Harlem or Dallas is guiding the other, and who knows which? This is D.J., Disc Jockey to America turning off. Vietnam, hot damn. (208)

This last question is not wholly rhetorical. For if the whole narrative is the imagining of that 'cripple Spade' (thus due to his disability a non-participant in the war), *Why Are We in Vietnam?* becomes an even more damning indictment of WASP America. D.J. is the ultimate 'white negro', the 'only American alive who could outtalk Cassius Clay' (22). Amongst Mailer's critics only one is prepared to allow this possibility. Barry H. Leeds suggests an implicit connection between author and black narrator – 'perhaps the most reasonable view is to see the Negro narrator as a metaphor for Mailer himself, a hip consciousness standing behind D.J., critical of Texas values and writing from New York'.[66] Certainly if Mailer had been seeking a critically detached viewpoint to put against D.J., perhaps only a black consciousness could have provided this. The novel was written from a background of racial violence, with riots throughout forty American cities in the summer of 1966. D.J. is WASP America as seen by Harlem, a point of view both culturally distinct from yet systematically persecuted by the entrenched racism of America's white majority.

D.J. is no more Mailer's voice than was Rojack. The most that could be said in either character's defence is that they are both victims as much as perpetrators of violence. Violence becomes their profoundest self-expression, but in no sense does Mailer condone the violence or the socio-political conditions producing it. With his distorted metaphysic ('God was a beast . . . and God said, "Go out and kill – fulfil my will, go and kill"' – 203) and his language of obscenity and technobabble, D.J. is Mailer's permutation on Burroughs's model of inhumanity. He introduces himself as having not only 'done animal murder' but 'murder of the soldierest sort' (7), a remark linking him with the unjust slaughtering in Vietnam. The psychiatrist's description of D.J. stresses his evil; he has 'read the Marquis de Sade at the age of fifteen' and is 'recalcitrant, charming, gracious, anti-Semitic, morally anesthetized, and smoldering with presumptive violence . . . murder configurations, suicide sets, disembowelment diagrams and diabolism designs' (14). He is a villain of America's own devising, born of the union between mankind and technology. We are right to see in him Mailer's fearful image of an America vicious and unhinged, a nation that 'refines perversity'[67] as does D.J., the 'genius philosopher and commo engineer . . . Grand Synthesizer of the Modern Void' (151–2).

The style of this novel becomes its political stance, and with Harlem rather than Dallas as its locus, Mailer's narrative takes its innovative place alongside the fiction of such white American writers as Carl Van Vechten and William Styron who, in their novels *Nigger Heaven* (1926) and *The Confessions of Nat Turner* (1966), also chose an African-American as narrator. D.J.'s main adversary is his father, Rusty Jethroe, a memorable portrait of American fascism as the type of the age, and in D.J.'s list of those bigotries which define Rusty's consciousness it is significant that the mix is unequivocally racist. The WASP patriarchy is being undermined by what Rusty sees as an unholy trinity of ideologies: Communism, feminism and ethnocentrism. Underlying all is the fear that white American male supremacy is losing its dominant hold over the majority. In Rusty's corporate brain the reasons are filed dogmatically, and amongst them are that 'the Yellow races are breaking loose', Africa is breaking loose', 'the white men are no longer champions in boxing', 'the great white athlete is being superseded by the great black athlete', and that 'Karate, a Jap sport, is now prerequisite to good street fighting' (110). Among his subscriptions to right-wing letterhead America it is significant that he pays dues to 'the Warren Commission Boosters'. One week after Kennedy's assassination, the Warren Commission was appointed by President Johnson to ascertain the facts concerning the killing. Ten months later it reported its findings, concluding that Lee Harvey Oswald acted alone in the assassination and that there were no grounds for any conspiracy theories. Yet by 1966, studies of the Commission were almost all describing its conclusions implausible and its investigations as 'extremely superficial'.[68] It was already acquiring a thoroughly discredited reputation and was very much in need of 'boosting'. Informed opinion then and since has continued to support the view that far from acting alone, Oswald was only the final, fatal link in a complex chain of anti-Kennedy prejudice. In a decade in which much American writing was concerned with conspiracy theories, concerned that the nation was controlled by unseen agencies and powers, Mailer here augments these anxieties. In Rusty, he satirises a hair-trigger reactionary, robotically conditioned to defend Americanism at all costs. D.J., looking into his father's eyes, sees there a reminder of 'his favorite theory which is that America is run by a mysterious hidden mastermind, a secret creature who's got a plastic asshole installed in his brain whereby he can shit out all his corporate management of thoughts' (36). In the novel's political allegory, Rusty is President Lyndon Johnson, most obvious in his fear-driven instinct to opt for a policy of overkill; he has the infamous air-raids made by the British on such German cities as Dresden in the Second World War as his strategic precedent ('the British were right . . . you don't pinpoint vital areas in a city, you blot it all out, you bury it deep in fire, shit, and fury' – 85). So, hunting for bear in the Alaskan wilderness the safari head guide, Big Luke Fellinka – General Westmoreland to Rusty's L.B.J. – is inclined to a 'military disposition. They must be in a position to bomb and superblast any grizzer who attacks' (116).

The novel's metaphysical climax is focused on its proposition that, with Vietnam as *quod erat demonstrandum*, America has taken the bestial for the celestial. This would be consistent with the Mailer theology, which in previous years he had been developing and amplifying in his non-fiction. According to this, God and Satan are locked in a battle for the soul of humanity, a version of the Manichean struggle, but with the outcome being dependent upon an individualistic ethic. Mailer has described himself as 'an existentialist who believes there is a God and a

Devil at war with one another'.[69] In a 1975 interview he explained that in his view God was not 'all-powerful: He's merely doing the best He can.'[70] The 'best He can' since God and the Devil become more or less powerful in proportion to the ethical performance of mankind in history. It is a theology which reinforces the view of Mailer as a moralist, however heterodox. 'What's significant is the idea that God is not all-powerful, nor the Devil. Rather it is that we exist as some mediating level between them. You see, this notion does restore a certain dignity to moral choice.'[71] In an age of moral decadence, and Mailer certainly regarded the 1960s as such, God's voice will become indistinguishable from that of his adversary.

The answer to the question put in the novel's title is to be found in this spiritual logic. In their climactic epiphany D.J. and Tex hear the Lord speak as the devil they and their nation have empowered, at loose in Vietnam and in their souls. Friendship is in confused flux with lust, murder and a bloody vitalism:

> Tex was ready to fight him to death, yeah, now it was there, murder between them under all friendship, for God was a beast, not a man, and God said, 'Go out and kill-fulfil my will, go and kill,' and they hung there each of them on the knife of the divide in all conflict of lust to own the other yet in fear of being killed by the other and as the hour went by and the lights shifted, something in the radiance of the North went into them, and owned their fear, some communion of telepathies and new powers, and they were twins, never to be near as lovers again, but killer brothers, *owned by something, prince of darkness, lord of light, they did not know* . . .
>
> (203–4 – my emphasis)

Here is manifest destiny misconstrued, American providence confused in the minds of its young warriors with 'the deep beast whispering fulfil my will, go forth and kill' (204). Yet the novel's final moments are also conscious of all that has been lost in the lives of an American generation unable to distinguish between the devil and the divine. In such moments Mailer reveals the

A Plunge into the Age

tragic vision he shares with the likes of Michael Herr, whose memoir of the war, *Dispatches* (1977), is also a lamentation for American idealism defiled:

> You'd stand nailed there in your tracks sometimes, no bearing and none in sight, thinking, *Where the fuck am I?*, fallen into some unnatural East–West interface, a California corridor cut and bought and burned deep into Asia, and once we'd done it we couldn't remember what for. . . . There was such a dense concentration of American energy there, American and essentially adolescent, if that energy could have been channelled into anything more than noise, waste and pain it would have lighted up Indochina for a thousand years.[72]

Many critics have noted the intertextuality of Mailer's novel, its awareness of such great antecedents of the American pastoral as Henry Thoreau's *Walden* and William Faulkner's *The Bear*. When it needs to, *Why Are We in Vietnam?* can also achieve a lyrical perception of the natural sublime, the momentary wonder of which stills and soothes the murdering will. In the twilight the two boys watch silently as a bull moose feeds at a salt-lick – a fearless King Moose gilded red by the sun and silvered by the moon, contentedly eating until he sees the boys' fire across the pond in the darkness:

> and he looked up and studied the fire some several hundred of feet away and gave a deep caw pulling in by some resonance of this grunt a herd of memories of animals at work and on the march and something gruff in the sharp wounded heart of things bleeding somewhere in the night, a sound somewhere in that voice in the North which spoke beneath all else to Ranald Jethroe Jellico Jethroe and his friend . . . (197)

The intimation received is in the end not one of transcendence, but of sorrow, inescapable and endemic. That is the meaning of the North American wilderness in Mailer's late-century reworking of its myth. The nation has slimed its very foundation in its embrace of technology for destruction. In Mailer's imagination of Vietnam, destruction has reached the ultimate of decreation, the undoing of God's work: 'We're destroying God's work, not man's work, but God's work.' From Vietnam to the Alaskan rim there is no peace, only 'the great sorrow up here brought by leaves and wind' and 'some speechless electric gathering of woe' (196).

5

From Egypt to Langley: *Ancient Evenings*, *Tough Guys Don't Dance* and *Harlot's Ghost*

It would be a further fifteen years before Mailer would publish his next novel, *Ancient Evenings* (1983). During the 1970s he consolidated his reputation both as a creative journalist and as a biographer of exceptional achievement in such works as *Of a Fire on the Moon* (1970) and *The Executioner's Song* (1979), with the latter winning Mailer's second Pulitzer Prize. He remained one of the most energetic contributors to the accelerating revision of American values, most famously perhaps in his response to Kate Millett's feminist attack upon him in her book *Sexual Politics* (1970). His published reply, *The Prisoner of Sex* (1971), was yet another extension of his literary range, being part polemic, part self-study, part literary criticism. Throughout these prolific years Mailer certainly justified Robert Lowell's description of him as 'the best journalist in America'[1] while at the same time raising doubts about his exhaustion as a writer of fiction. Yet as far back as 1964 he had begun to promise delivery of a novel of the highest quality, one that would establish him without question as a literary artist of the first rank.

Walter Minton, who had been president of Putnam's Sons, Mailer's publishers from 1955 to 1963, recalls reading an early fragment, 'maybe 70 pages of the big novel that eventually became *Ancient Evenings* many, many years ago, sometime around 1964';[2] this would be consistent with Mailer's first published reference to the idea of such a novel, at the close of *Advertisements for Myself* (1959). The passage played a significant part in the mythology of the Mailer ego as he raised the stakes and with a swaggering baseball metaphor set himself a target which may have been just too high:

> If it is to have any effect, and I can hardly look forward to exhausting the next ten years without hope of a deep explosion of effect, the book will be fired to its fuse by the rumour that once I pointed to the farthest fence and said that within ten years I would try to hit the longest ball ever to go up into the accelerated hurricane air of our American letters.[3]

It was not ten but almost twenty years before he eventually delivered the completed book to its publishers, Little, Brown, on 1 August 1982. He had worked intermittently on what came to be known as 'the Egyptian novel' for at least ten years, and certainly throughout the 1970s. The novel was to be the first in a trilogy, though this idea faded out by the mid-1980s.[4] Certainly by 1982 the publishing world was willing to pay unprecedentedly high prices for the rights to *Ancient Evenings*, knowing that if Mailer could match his recent success with *The Executioner's Song* in this much-anticipated novel, he would indeed have succeeded in hitting that longest ball in American literature. At home, Little, Brown had already paid $1 million for the rights to the novel – as early as 1974. At that time this was a record fee, though by 1980 they increased this to $4 million as their accepted bid for rights to the proposed trilogy. In Britain Macmillan offered $120,000 for the rights to the novel, sight unseen.

With such hype preceding it, *Ancient Evenings* was finally published in the spring of 1983. By May of that year it was showing as sixth on the *New York Times* best-seller list, and it remained on the list for a further fifteen weeks. It was the author's prediction that the novel would 'get the best and worst reviews'[5] received by any of his books, and indeed its reviews ranged from the mocking and vicious, to others which saw it as a formidable achievement, a work of unique vision and quality. Mailer and his publishers exploited the controversy with a tactic they had used previously in publicising his biography of Marilyn Monroe: a poster of some of the novel's worse notices was compiled, these being set alongside similar attacks nineteenth-century reviewers had made upon European and American literary works now accepted as classics. With the poster's borders reading 'plus ça change, plus c'est la même chose' and with a bold headline of 'HIDEOUS REVIEWS', potential buyers of *Ancient Evenings* were reminded that a sour review has often been the fate of a classic unappreciated in its day. Thus if sections of Mailer's novel seemed hopelessly clotted and turgid, so the reviewer of Herman Melville's nineteenth-century masterpiece *Moby Dick* was compelled to draw attention to that novel's 'dreariness' in parts. And if Walt Whitman's great volume of poems, *Leaves of Grass*, could be dismissed on publication as 'a mass of stupid filth' so also might Mailer's novel, in one reviewer's view so much 'holistic poop', eventually transcend such reductive nonsense.[6]

A decade later, *Ancient Evenings* seems to have hardly created that 'deep explosion of effect' its author had hoped for at its conception. In these years there have been only three extended critical essays on the novel.[7] One of these, noting the critics' silence, suggests that without any 'authoritative, detailed studies of *Ancient Evenings* . . . there is every sign that the critical community remains baffled' by it.[8] Perhaps, but I think it more likely that the novel is still regarded as both *outré* and so resistant to category as to subvert any substantial critical appraisal of it. Such a reputation, together with the novel's formidable length, means that we have a novel unread rather than one unvalued. Mailer himself recognised this; speaking in 1987 he told his interviewer, 'one of the things that startled me was how few people ever made any attempt to read *Ancient Evenings*. Even people who love my work just said, "Well, gee, I couldn't get into it".'[9] As one of the novel's reviewers predicted, 'Mailer is sure to catch hell for this demanding book',[10] though as the years go by and the demands are so rarely taken up by readers, *Ancient Evenings*, masterpiece or not, has been consigned not so much to hell as the purgatory of neglect.

My own view coincides broadly with that of Mary Lee Settle, whose review for the *Los Angeles Times* raises the crucial issue of the reader's consent as a prerequisite for admission to the novel's pleasures:

> I know of no other modern works that so successfully evoke the pre-Judeo-Christian era, before magic yielded to morals except Marguerite Yourcenar's *Hadrian* and Fellini's 'Satyricon' film. . . . *Ancient Evenings* goes beyond them into a language and a world that is more alien, but alien only until we consent to go there, and when we do the reward is great. Every object is permeated with magic. That glimpsed area is evoked where changes of images, faces, places are as familiar as the nightly approach of dreams. . . . Huge in scope, magnificent as fiction, luxuriant and wise, this is Mailer's finest and most courageous book.[11]

While there are certainly sections of the novel that are not only far from 'magnificent as fiction' but closer to miserable, such passages are, as Richard Poirier argues, typical in 'books of sustained visionary ambition' which like '*Paradise Lost* or *Moby Dick* are bound to have stretches of tiresome exposition' in them.[12] Accepting this, the reader is more than compensated for the tedium of Mailer's fifth chapter, 'The Book of Queens', by many other successes such as the epic Battle of Kadesh or the young Menenhetet's remembrances of the Pharaoh's court, which both in sweep and telling detail achieve that magical transport described by Mary Lee Settle.

Though often criticised for over-writing in both *Ancient Evenings* and *Harlot's Ghost*, in the former the length of the novel is necessary 'to give a sense of the pace . . . of ancient Egypt' as Mailer saw it.[13] Indeed, no extract can possibly do justice to the magnificent cumulative effects of his imagery in many places in this novel. In such places Mailer demonstrates his reach as a truly imaginative writer after a decade of inspiring journalism. The novel is, in Harold Bloom's words, nothing if not 'an extravagant invention',[14] or as another reviewer put it, 'a huge act of imagining'.[15] In his challenging, almost disdainful address to his reader's imagination, Mailer is most clearly in full possession of his vision:

> Try then to look into the blinding light that came from the gold and silver hull of a state barge of the King being rowed upstream with a group of royal officials to take on Pharaoh's duties in towns to the South. They stood beside a huge altar of gold in the stern . . . a gift no doubt from Ramses Nine to one of His temples . . . and I thought the state barge looked like the golden bark of Ra being rowed across the sky even as it went by the bend in the glare of the sun. It was the grandest sight I had ever seen on the river, but I was to witness a greater one in the next hour when we came to the outskirts of Memphi.[16]

And so the narration goes on, adding image upon extraordinary image, a voluptuous exploration of a milieu almost beyond history, all mediated through a narrative consciousness which is itself both in and out of time.

This is not a novel which either lends itself to quick summary or encourages it. It is very much more than an 'historical novel' and to say its setting is that of Egypt's New Kingdom in its nineteenth and twentieth dynasties (1570–1090 BC) is to simplify Mailer's complex narrative approach. This comprises a magical enterprise of memory, telepathy and what can only be called supernatural cognition, emanating from Menenhetet II, an Egyptian nobleman. Having been murdered at the age of twenty-one, his narrative makes *Ancient Evenings* perhaps the longest ghost-story ever told, for his is a consciousness on the cusp between death and reincarnation. As the narrative opens we, along with Menenhetet II, experience all the primordial dread of his ultimate journey beyond mortality – 'Crude thoughts and fierce forces are my state. I do not know who I am. Nor what I was. I cannot hear a sound. Pain is near that will be like no pain felt before' (3). This voice is a subtle shadow of the young man who was Menenhetet II, his shade or, as Mailer (following Egyptian mythology) prefers, his Ka, which stumbles forward through this frightening underworld, the Land of the Dead. It is there that we meet for the first time the Ka of Menenhetet I, who had been in life the great-grandfather of the young man, and whose experiences through four reincarnations will be the main substance of *Ancient Evenings*. Through such involutions in its narrative form (Menenhetet I and the story of his previous lives are told to the Pharaoh Ramses IX, in the presence of the six-year-old Menenhetet II, though the reader is never allowed to forget the ghostliness of this text, sent to us from the Land of the Dead) as well as in its thematic substance, the novel is an audacious imagining of the world beyond appearances.

Mailer's intentions were both original and far-reaching, to create as he put it 'a new psychology, a new consciousness . . . I was trying to write of these matters from the perspective of those times'.[17] And in 1993 he told me that in *Ancient Evenings* he was 'trying to write a novel that would exist in the past and have no relations to the present'.[18] His narrative succeeds in situating the reader as an intimate insider of the courts of two Pharaohs, Ramses II and Ramses IX, while also having us occupy, with the Ka of Menenhetet II, a transcendent position of terrifying detachment. For beyond the daily lives of these Egyptians, high or low-born, lies their ultimate subtext, the Book of the Dead which told of their duad, the climactic encounters with the monsters lying in wait beyond the tomb. Only by passing through such perils could they hope to reach their heavenly resurrection.

In both *An American Dream* and *Why Are We in Vietnam?*, Mailer had given every sign of being engaged with the mystical, with the penetration of quotidian reality *by* the mystical, in a dramatisation of what Peter Brooks once called 'the moral occult'. In his essay 'The Melodramatic Imagination' (1972), Brooks placed Mailer as the latest in a line of European and American authors whose work used 'the things and gestures of the real world, of social life as kinds of metaphors which refer us to the realm of spiritual reality, the realm of latent moral meanings':[19]

The melodramatic imagination is, then, perhaps a way of perceiving and imaging the spiritual in a world where there is no longer any clear idea of the sacred . . . where the body of the ethical has become a sort of *deus absconditus* which must be sought for, posited, brought into man's existence through exercise of the spiritualist imagination. Balzac's and James's melodrama, and the development of the melodramatic mode from, say, Samuel Richardson to Norman Mailer, is perhaps first of all a desperate effort to renew contact with the sacred *through* the representation of fallen reality, to insist that behind reality, hidden by it yet indicated within it, there is a realm where large moral forces are operative, where large choices of ways of being must be made. I have called this realm the moral occult: it is occult in a world where there is no clear system of sacred myth, no unity of belief, no accepted metaphorical chain leading from the phenomenal to the spiritual, only a fragmented society and fragments of myths. Yet the most Promethean of modern writers insist that this realm does exist, and write their fictions to make it exist, to show its primacy in life.[20]

Brooks's perceptive comments were made long before the appearance of *Ancient Evenings*, though there seems little doubt he would not have been surprised by Mailer's embrace of the gnostic in his chosen setting and subject.

In both of his previous novels, Mailer's representation of the moral occult led him to stretch the boundaries of realism, some felt beyond their breaking-point. Certainly a character such as Rojack is in desperate struggle with what seem to him demons and gods most palpable, his high-wire walk along Kelly's parapet being offered as an act of both spiritual expiation and dragon-slaying. In *Ancient Evenings* Mailer is liberated from dependency upon such symbolic devices. Egyptian culture furnished him with a model of a world permeated by sacred myth, with a unity of belief and an accepted metaphorical chain leading from the phenomenal to the spiritual. The world of the pharaohs and their subjects provided him with a metaphysic which assumed the fundamental, inextricable relationship between humanity and the divine. All of this must have come as a release from the burdens of addressing America's cynicism throughout the 1970s. For his critique of postwar America is rooted very largely in his attack upon its secularism; his often-voiced contempt for 'technologyland' is not so much Luddite as evangelical in origin. In America the 1970s were characterised by a sense of intellectual exhaustion, by ideological demoralisation and pessimism. For Mailer the possibility of realising that 'revolution in the consciousness of our time' must have seemed increasingly remote. With *Ancient Evenings* as 'Mailer's ur-text for the 1970s'[21] we can now see that he had all but abandoned his high-profile politics of the previous decade to exercise instead that 'spiritualist imagination' of reality and public events so well described by Peter Brooks. This can be seen in all of his published work of the 1970s, to varying degrees. In, for instance, *The Fight* (1975) his perceptions are often filtered through an imagination which takes account of the 'moral occult'. So, in Zaïre watching Muhammed Ali pretend to take a fall in a pre-fight sparring match, Mailer is more than willing to read the event through African eyes:

> The Africans in the rear of the hall were stricken. A silence, not without dread, was rising from them. Nobody believed Ali had been hurt – they were afraid of something worse. By way of this charade, Ali had given a tilt to the field of forces surrounding the fight. Like a member of a chorus had he offered the comment: 'He's had his mouth shut for the last time.' The African audience reacted uneasily, as if his words could excite unseen forces. There was hardly a Zairois in the audience who did not know that Mobutu, good president, was not only a dictator but a doctor of the occult with a pygmy for his own private conjurer. . . . If, however, Mobutu had his *feticheur*, who among these Africans would not believe Ali was also a powerful voice in the fearful and magical zone between the living and the dead?[22]

And in this book's final paragraph Mailer returns to 'the play of forces between those who are living and those who are dead'.

Some of the best writing in *Ancient Evenings* finds itself in this field, in for instance Menenhetet's memory of the Battle of Kadesh where the warrior-pharaoh Ramses II leads the Egyptian armies to victory over the Hittites. Whereas Mailer has always seen America as tragically thwarted in its cultural development, self-divided, its history showing that fatal split between 'two rivers' so that 'there was nothing in our growth which was organic',[23] his vision of Egypt in the reign of Ramses II is one of wholeness and harmony. Ramses is defined by that sacred unity of body and spirit, substance and decoration which typify the organic integration Mailer most admires. His virtues are almost always couched in terms of harmony, as in Menenhetet's first description of him as 'beautiful in the way twenty birds are one bird in the instant they turn' (251). Throughout the Battle of Kadesh, Ramses comports himself with the courage and dignity of one mandated by the gods, and again the whole picture is threaded by the leitmotiv of harmony as, for instance, in the extraordinary night-scene after victory has been won. Here, Ramses II undertakes the grisly ceremony of receiving, one by one, the thousands of severed hands of the slain Hittites as the ultimate proof of victory. After the *Sturm und Drang* of the bloody conflict the warrior-king is now transfigured in quiet, godlike ascendancy:

> All through the night, our fires burned, and through the same night, Usermare-Setpenere stood in His Chariot under a full moon and received the severed hands of the slain Hittites one by one. . . . I realised once again how to be near Him was to gain all knowledge of how a God might act when He is in the form of a man. He looks so much like a man and yet reveals divinity by even the smallest of His moves. In this case, it was that He did not move His feet . . . an exhibition of such poise that one saw the mark of a God . . . these hands were added to the pile in a harmony between the height and the base that was equal to the harmony with which our Ramses received His soldiers. (355–6)

In Mailer's vision, Ramses II is an heroic paradigm for that inextricable connection between the Egyptians, nature and their wondrous gods, for a culture in harmony with its sources and surroundings, both natural and supernatural.

In the light of this novel's preoccupation with the theme of the afterlife and reincarnation, it should not surprise us that this was also central to Mailer's response to Gary Gilmore, the murderer whose life and death are the subject of the 'true life novel' *The Executioner's Song* (1979). Gilmore believed passionately in reincarnation, though with the stress on an active rather than passive spirit. Of his own imminent death Gilmore said, 'I just think it will be familiar . . . I must keep my mind singular and strong – In death you can choose in a way that you can't choose in life. The biggest mistake you could make when you die is to be afraid.'[24] But Mailer's own views on this matter go back at least as far as the early 1960s. In 'The Eleventh Presidential Paper-Death' (1963), he offers a critique of European existentialism on the grounds that neither of its two major exponents, Heidegger or Sartre, were willing to extend the existential commitment beyond death:

> Existentialism is rootless unless one dares the hypothesis that death is an existential continuation of life, that the soul may either pass through migrations, or cease to exist in the continuum of nature . . . accepting this hypothesis, authenticity and commitment return to the center of ethics, for man then faces no peril so huge as alienation from his own soul, a death which is other than death, a disappearance into nothingness rather than into Eternity.[25]

At the end of *Ancient Evenings* we leave Menenhetet II engaged in just such a struggle; in this sense the novel offers an unequivocally positive resolution in its vision of immortal striving. When, after 700 pages, Menenhetet's tale comes full circle and we are with him and his great-grandfather as they navigate towards the Last Bend of the Duad, where 'Anubis weighs the heart of him who will be judged' (703), our imaginative involvement is thorough. Mailer's vision is sustained through the supply of fine detail (according to Poirier, Mailer's researches for the novel were 'encyclopaedic' and were said to have included 'a total absorption of the Egyptian funerary literature called the Book of the Dead'[26]) which mixes both conventional images of Inferno ('I saw the Ka of all who were so unfortunate as to be the enemies of Ra, and witnessed the destruction of their bodies at the First Gate, and the loss of their shadows as they fell into pits of fire' – 701) with an Egyptian iconography of Apocalypse:

> In the Sixth Bend of the Duad, I saw a God with the head of a fish, and He could pacify monsters of the sea by shaking out a net to His own powerful incantation. He knew the genius of the net and how to tie knots that would confound monsters . . . and in the Seventh and Last Bend we even passed by the monster who is named Ammit, and He is the Eater of the Dead and usually rests at the side of the scales while Anubis weighs the heart of him who will be judged. (702–3)

To know that Ammit is 'usually' found by the side of the scales is reassuring! Yet we are finally brought to consider that *Ancient Evenings* is, however, not a novel about gods or those would be gods, but about the need for invoking our human potentialities. Mailer once lamented that to live in the contemporary United States was to live in a 'rootless moral wilderness,'[27] and in this novel he succeeded in representing the cultural antithesis of that condition, for Menenhetet II eventually understands that 'there is no loneliness . . . that is worse than being ignorant of the worth of your soul'. Instead of a moral wilderness, ancient Egypt exists beneath an inescapable canopy of supernatural force to which all know they will be answerable.

This is the novel's fundamental given, and it releases Menenhetet II into his deepest knowledge: that only by opening the heart to others can the human spirit hope 'to reach the heavens of highest endeavor' (707), and so discover its true worth. In the last moments of his narrative he is able to see his great-grandfather as no longer an 'absurd old man' but as a spirit connatural:

> His body had reeked of the Land of the Dead . . . and now I perceived that in his loneliness, he wished for me to join him. The tales he had told our Pharaoh, had been told for me as

well. It was I whom he wanted to trust him. And I did. Here in the Duad, in this hour, I would trust him. (708)

And with this resolution there is a commingling of spirit as the thrice-reincarnated Menenhetet I expires and invests 'the power of his heart' in the Ka of Menenhetet II. *Ancient Evenings* closes with this new life-force in a still-indeterminate condition, awaiting its destiny which, in Mailer's original plan, would have been developed in the second book of the trilogy – 'and so I do not know if I will labor in greed forever among the demonic or serve some noble purpose I cannot name' (709). Yet though that specific destiny is unknown, Mailer's final chapter allows Menenhetet II some purchase on the world he will be reborn into. This will be a Graeco-Roman prototype of the modern, a world fallen into a degraded sense of the sacred. As old Menenhetet laments, 'for our Land of the Dead now belongs to them, and the Greeks think no more of it than a picture that is seen on the wall of a cave' (705).

Mailer's eighth novel, *Tough Guys Don't Dance* (1984), was another book he produced in a rush, 'a commercial quickie' as one reviewer put it.[28] It took Mailer just two months to write, though he had been trying to make a start 'for about a year'[29] previously. With a contractual deadline approaching fast, the novel's composition has more than a little in common with the pressured delivery of *An American Dream*. The two novels have, indeed, often been compared, though few would agree with Leo Lerman who sees it as 'a mature *An American Dream*'.[30] More accurately, Michael Ventura draws the parallel as 'an overworked rehash of the critically savaged, badly underrated *An American Dream*'.[31] Those who value the novel usually regard it as yet another expression of the author's diverse literary repertoire, seeing it as a talented pastiche of the hard-boiled genre associated with the psychological thrillers of Dashiell Hammett or James M. Cain. Mailer himself acknowledged the novel's limitations, attributing these to necessary expediency:

In movie-making . . . they have a wonderful phrase: 'Do what is necessary,' and what that means is, we'll get the shot in whether it's good or it's bad. We'll have it by dark because otherwise we're lost. *Tough Guys* is an example of what happens when you have to do what is necessary.[32]

And speaking in 1991, he followed the prevailing critical view, referring to *Tough Guys* as 'probably the weakest of all' his novels.[33] Still, while 'it could have been a disaster' due to the rushed pace of its delivery, it is in the end only what he termed 'a small failure'.[34]

'The least of his novels',[35] 'the weakest of his only-kidding books'[36] – these are the judgements applied almost invariably by the novel's critics. Wilfrid Sheed sums up its wasted exuberance as akin to 'a powerful machine that has spun out of control and is careering off the walls of the lab. After a while you stop expecting anything great from it and just wait for it to run down.'[37] *Tough Guys* is certainly not the novel to which new readers should turn for purchase on Mailer's claims to seriousness, for though some of his famous themes do appear along the way, they are subordinated to the need to keep the pot boiling at all costs. The novel is, at most, an opportunity for the writer to demonstrate his stylistic flair. In this area he achieves a good deal, fashioning a plot so wildly baroque and an atmosphere so thoroughly *noir* with its fogs, headless corpses and pervasive sleaze such as to suggest the burlesque. There is an unembarrassed willingness to take on a racy pulp style and thereby prove a point to those who had condemned his previous novel for what they saw as its gratuitous length. Perhaps, as Walter Anderson put it, Mailer 'had set out to demonstrate that he too could write a page-turner, as if responding to the criticism of *Ancient Evenings*'.[38]

This would be the most positive view on *Tough Guys*, to see it as a work having its fun with the conventions of genre fiction, fulfilling a contractual obligation with his publishers, while at the same time allowing the author to show that he could produce a novel of a sort utterly unlike its predecessor, with its alleged faults. For if we do look for 'anything great' in it, our search would certainly be forlorn. The novel's first-person narrator, Tim Madden, is surely Mailer's most miserable hero, without Rojack's vivid sense of purpose or even O'Shaugnessy's simplistic idealism. In the Epilogue we are left with nothing but Madden's unregenerate bad faith. There, at least, we remember the novel's epigraph – 'there are mistakes too monstrous for remorse':

> And I? Well, I am so compromised by so many acts that I must try to write my way out of the internal prison of my nerves, my guilts and my deep-rooted spiritual debts. Yet I would take the chance again. In truth, it is not all bad. Madeleine and I sleep for hours with our arms around each other. I live within the fold of her deed, not uncomfortable and not insecure, deeply attached to her and aware that all my present stability of mind rests on the firm foundation of a mortal crime.[39]

Faced by the absurd proliferation of corpses – beneath the waves, the beaches and supporting, it seems, the very foundations of Provincetown (Mailer's evocation of place, the *genius loci* of this remote coastal community, has much in common with the gothic *mise-en-scène* we are introduced to at the start of *Harlot's Ghost*, and both supply exact correlatives for the narrator's mental state. Ever since Mount Anaka and its island fastness defined the soldierly psyche in *The Naked and the Dead*, Mailer has integrated character and place to memorable effect) – it comes as little surprise to hear Madden's nostrum: 'with anger such as ours, murder – most terrifying to say – could prove the cure for all the rest' (223). In his narrative 'all the rest' comprises a sink of degraded hopes, ending up with his failed marriage to *femme fatale* Patty Lareine. Together these two contrive their own version of an internecine *grand guignol*, living 'for years on such an edge' (223) of anger and sudden violence that one is not surprised by all that rushes in to fill the void of Patty's death. When he asks himself, 'how many times over these last few years had I come to the edge of battering Patty Lareine with my bare hands?' (159), we cannot suppose that his story will be one tempered by reason. *Tough Guys* consists of Madden's life of anguished confusion, a narrative that begins in the 'misery, self-pity and despair' (10) of their separation, all too graphically revealed when he discovers his wife's severed head. Beginning in that despair, his story becomes an extensive record of human degradation relieved only by the reader's suspicion, perhaps even hope, that the whole novel is indeed 'only kidding'.

One of the most disappointing aspects of the novel is its willingness to exploit for quick effect some all-too-familiar Maileresque themes. In his introduction to *Some Honorable Men*, a collection of his essays on American political conventions, he writes that 'if there is one fell rule in art it is that repetition kills the soul'.[40] Yet it would be difficult to point to any issue or theme in *Tough Guys* that is not a trivialised reinscription of concerns which once had philosophical integrity in Mailer's previous work. Such themes as the demonology of dread (which received its first, and memorable exploration in Rojack's journey along Kelly's parapet) are here potted in a rhetoric that congeals – 'the importance of the journey must be estimated by my dread of doing it' (83). All is fodder to a writer looking for expedient means to 'do what was necessary' to complete the novel on time. So Madden's father, after taking 'a big belt of his watered bourbon', lets go a bolt of pure Mailerese – 'Schizophrenics in looney bins only get cancer half as often as the average population . . . cancer is the cure for schizophrenia. Schizophrenia is the cure for cancer' (158–9). Throughout the 1960s Mailer's critique of American culture had been fired by a canon of essays wherein the notion of a cancered body politic had been a metaphor of central force. In Dougy Madden's mouth the idea is as watered down as the bourbon. Certainly *Tough Guys* was not the novel to provide the context for radical thematic innovation, but to defend it on the grounds of its being a lively genre pastiche means that any expectations of originality are surrendered to the comic compensations of parody. Yet it *is* dismaying to discover the ease with which in this novel Mailer's fundamental themes are themselves made parodic.

* * *

If *Tough Guys Don't Dance* shows many signs of being a rushed job, no one could accuse Mailer of rushing though his most recent novel, *Harlot's Ghost*, seven years in the writing. He gave a number of interviews to coincide with the British publication of the novel in 1991, and at the first of these I asked him to speak about the extent to which the new novel addressed one of his abiding political concerns, that of totalitarianism in American life. His reply to the question was rather indirect, though informative:

> America is a democracy ... you have close to absolute freedom of expression in America. Nonetheless, we're an immensely manipulative country. Anthony Burgess gave me a nice review of *Harlot's Ghost* and at the end of it he said something to the effect that there might be something in the novel for all us 'lowly governed', and I was taken with the phrase because that's what we are in America – we're the lowly governed. It doesn't matter how much influence we have, unless we have direct influence with the Establishment, with the ongoing political Establishment, we have no influence at all. They go ahead and do what they need to do, what they want to do. And I felt for a long time that the Cold War has been a most useful fiction for America for at least the last 30 years – I'd say since 1960 there wasn't a time when the Russians weren't ready to make peace, because they recognised that this Cold War was absolutely wrecking their economic system, and I think in America the cold calculation was made – 'we can afford it and they can't, so let's keep upping the ante'. Over and over and over again in our history there were places where the Cold War could have been defused, and we failed to do it ... during all of this the CIA was our ideological arm, and I thought it was worth doing a book in great detail about how those people worked because you know it's always fun to do a novel when you essentially respect the people you're writing about, but they're engaged in the wrong activity. It gives you ironies that you really can play with as you write, and you discover things as you write. It's always interesting

to write upon the lip of a paradox, because the paradox quivers, and lo and behold you discover something new.[41]

Though he seems to speak critically in the above excerpt in his remarks about the disempowered and 'lowly governed', his attitude to the CIA in *Harlot's Ghost* is at best ambiguous. His reference to CIA staff as people he can 'essentially respect' even while 'they're engaged in the wrong activity' recalls the ambiguous portrait of both Croft and Cummings in *The Naked and the Dead*. The fact is that Mailer has for long been in his own words 'a left conservative',[42] and obsessed by the Establishment ever since he attended Harvard. His writing, since *The Executioner's Song* in 1979 and continuing through *Ancient Evenings*, has also eschewed any explicit political stance. The novel's genre is at least partly that of a history novel, a genre Mailer seems to have understood as conferring a kind of political neutrality upon the narrative – 'there is nothing I can do about these events any more. I have the detachment of the past. You get angry and strident when you can change something. Here [in *Harlot's Ghost*] I just thought I should try to understand them.'[43]

Harlot's Ghost does not set out to be, then, a critique of the CIA, and indeed Mailer's attitude to the organisation appears to be one of observational detachment. Many readers of his work, particularly those familiar with the politically engaged writing of the 1960s, will perhaps be surprised by this. Some of his very best writing has seen him as an historian of the present in such books as *The Armies of the Night* and *Of a Fire on the Moon*, but in *Harlot's Ghost* he turns away from history-making to accept the immutable record of the past – 'there is nothing I can do about these events any more'. As one of the novel's reviewers put it, 'Mailer does not use history but succumbs to it.'[44] The revisionist view of history seems not to have occurred to him; nor, unless his remarks above are to be understood ironically, has he seen just how the imaginative history that is *Harlot's Ghost* does itself contribute to an altered consciousness of, say, the Bay of Pigs crisis.

Reviews of the novel were predictably scathing about its length:

When Mailer's publisher mailed me a typescript of the book, it arrived in a box so large I thought someone had sent me 50 Indian River grapefruits . . . a novel so immense that Jacob Epstein, Random House's editorial director, asked him to bring it to an end so that it could be bound using existing technology.[45]

Called variously 'a humongous counter-history of the CIA'[46] and a novel that confronts its reader with the 'gruelling ordeal . . . of beating his way through its punishing prolixity',[47] some of Mailer's reviewers were not pleased to discover the 'mind-boggling immensity'[48] of the book they had to review. As with *Ancient Evenings* the reviews were mixed. Whereas some saw the novel's concluding words 'to be continued' as a 'terrifying promise' to which the only response could be 'God forbid',[49] others looked forward to the arrival of the sequel – 'if part two of *Harlot's Ghost*, whose last words are "To be continued", were available today, I'd gladly read on'.[50] In general the American reviews were more favourable than the British, with among the most interesting exceptions to the latter being those of two novelists, Anthony Burgess and Salman Rushdie. Both saw considerable value in the novel and were certainly able to overcome objections to its word count. Burgess opens his review with the suggestion that Mailer and Tolstoy can stand comparison ('Tolstoy's ghost haunts America, and . . . Mailer is the man to lay it')[51] and concludes it with a further allusion to Mailer's place among the nineteenth-century masters of the realist novel – 'he reminds us, as Balzac and Dickens do, that the novel is more than diversion. *Harlot's Ghost* is to be read in the White House as well as in Langley, and it ought to be pored over in the sancta of our own MI6.'[52]

Mailer seemed determined to play down such higher meanings, however, remarking that he had in the past believed that 'the CIA was the most sinister organization we have, but I came to think it was the most sinister bureaucracy – and my novel became a comedy of manners'.[53] This latter description is a key to the author's approach to his subject, for it is style rather than political substance that fascinates him here. It is the Ivy League

WASPs with their inbred feel for protocol and caste who rule Mailer's blue-blooded CIA. Thus if Hugh Montague, alias 'Harlot', has all the hauteur of a CIA patriarch, so his godson and eventual cuckolder, the novel's narrator Herrick 'Harry' Hubbard, finds that his life in the Company is in large part an education in social standing. At dinner with the CIA Chief-of-Staff in Montevideo, E. Howard Hunt (Hunt was the real-life CIA propaganda officer during the Bay of Pigs operation), Hubbard is already beginning to take the measure of his own social reach:

> Even when we were only three for dinner, our setting was formal. At their long handsome table, Howard always sat at one end and Dorothy at the other. If he and she were absolute snobs, I was learning none-the-less that to be accepted by such people is not unlike receiving an award; one is bathed in balmy waters ... Howard did not yet comprehend the impossibility of certain social desires. I believe one reason I liked him was that I often felt more than equal to him. (471)

The novel's title owes a debt to Balzac's novel *A Harlot High and Low*, which was also the title of an essay Mailer wrote in 1976. In a letter of 1994 Mailer confirmed my view that in its concern with the CIA as the covert 'mind of America' and the special experience of the spy as one who must transcend existential norms – living with and within multiple identities in order to function and survive – this essay is a distinct foreshadowing of the themes of *Harlot's Ghost*. 'Altogether, *Harlot's Ghost* is, of course, more grounded in the stuff than the essay, but yes', he told me,[54] his attraction to the CIA as a subject had its first extended consideration in the essay 'A Harlot High and Low':

> Whores and political agents made a fair association for Balzac. The harlot, after all, inhabited the world of *as if*. You paid your money and the harlot acted for a little while ... *as if* she loved you, and that was a more mysterious proposition than one would think, for it is always mysterious to play a role. It is equal in a sense to living under cover.[55]

The prostituting of the self in the service of an ideological client, and the professional embrace of a perilous make-believe are only two of the links that struck Mailer in his choice of a title for the novel. Beyond this the novel takes as a core theme the issue of identity, already a generic motif in novels of espionage and for long one of Norman Mailer's bailiwicks. One has only to consider the manifold identities unfolding throughout *Ancient Evenings* or the problematising of identity in *An American Dream* to see that agents, double agents and the pathology of the spy can easily be accommodated within a lifelong concern. Mailer acknowledges the autobiographical roots of this theme:

> I have an umbilical connection to *Harlot's Ghost* because I've been obsessed with questions of identity all of my life. . . . I had my identity forcibly changed at the age of 25, when I went from being an unknown writer to a public writer in a month . . . so I've always been fascinated with spies and actors and people who take on roles that are not their own and then take on that role more than they might like to.[56]

For a writer of Mailer's ambition, the CIA offered a commensurate subject, its influence vast and all-pervasive. 'There was, after all, a vision', he wrote in 'A Harlot High and Low', a vision which would encompass all intelligence so that 'there was no natural end to the topics the CIA could legitimately interest itself in'.[57] To know the CIA would be to know America, its interstices and arteries. Servicing the system were its operatives, a polymathic élite who were to be 'an order of potential martyrs to Henry Luce's American Century'.[58] Their special appeal to Mailer however, lay not in any *esprit de corps*, but rather in their unique existential experience transcending self and identity: in this regard if no other the CIA agent would embody a superhuman mentality capable of efficient function in a divided postwar world. Inside and out, the paradigm was one of confounding division, with 'the human brain divided: into a right lobe and a left lobe; a bold side and a cautious one; a moralist and a sinner; a radical and a conservative . . . We are all ourselves, and to some degree we are the opposite of ourselves.'[59] The heroism of the spy is defined by his ability to find the authentic action amidst 'the confusion of enigmatic projects and multiple identities in order to give the country what it really needs, that is, what he believes America secretly desires'.[60] One can see in such passages that what drew Mailer's interest was a drama of personality and that such themes – of the significance of the CIA to American postwar history, and the idea of the CIA agent as an existentially heroic subject – were central to the conception of *Harlot's Ghost*.

As Anthony Burgess remarked, 'we may not speak of a plot in so discursive a work: plots, yes, a single narrative thread, no'.[61] Of those reviews that found fault with the novel, most did so on structural grounds. The novel can be divided into two main sections, an opening section, the Omega manuscript, consisting of 100 or so pages which takes place in 1983 and which one might call the time-present of Harry Hubbard's life, and the major part of his narrative, the Alpha manuscript. This is a retrospective account of his early years in the CIA from 1956 to 1963. Stated this way, one can see that the narrative from 1963 to 1983 is, in effect, missing from the chronology. Into this substantial lacuna Mailer's reviewers gazed incredulously, having read in excess of 1000 pages to find the novel still unfinished. Wrath ensued and the novel was condemned for structural incoherence. The author tried to stay ahead of the criticism by representing the 'missing' section as an unappreciated virtue of *Harlot's Ghost*. 'I regard this book as a novel with a legitimate architecture – but one with an excluded middle':

> The reader, having been given the end and the beginning will conceive of that 'middle'; they know that the middle takes place in Vietnam, and Watergate, and that the love affair between Harry Hubbard and Kittredge Gardiner Montague was consummated in that 'middle', and they will think about it, and in their own mind – if they like the book – they'll come to the point where they begin to conceive of that middle novel. Now, if I come along and write it in the next few years, they'll then be able to check their version of the novel against mine.[62]

Mailer's 'gentle reader' would have to be very gentle indeed to indulge in the sort of imaginative collaboration envisaged here. It is much more likely that the reader will share at least some of the reviewers' irritation when deprived of the narrative closure so long anticipated. In his review of the novel, Wilfrid Sheed argues that '*Harlot's Ghost* would not be the first book to contain a disastrous structural flaw . . . and the many excellent pages of this one should not be buried under its mistakes.'[62] Those readers prepared to wait another seven years for the sequel may also wish to know that, as Sheed writes, Mailer's 'own interest in resolving his story may be divined from his announcement that he plans to dash off a book about Picasso before he gets around to it'.[64] The fact is that *Harlot's Ghost* is not a self-contained novel, and that Mailer's notion of a deliberately 'excluded middle' section appears just a little sophistical.

Another main reason why many readers might regret that the narrative never returns to conclude the Omega manuscript is that this first section offers some of the best writing in the entire novel. Here, in what *Time* magazine called 'a burst of bravura storytelling',[65] we are introduced to some of the novel's leading players, to Harry Hubbard as he drives back through the cold March mists to his ancestral home on an island off the Maine seacoast, and to Harry's wife Kittredge who was formerly the wife of Hugh Montague, the CIA's 'Harlot'. By the end of this Omega section we have been treated to Harry's predilection for the gothic in storytelling. Like his author, Harry is prepared to entertain the notion of a world beyond the human; his recollections are permeated by his occult sensibility which is, perhaps, the perfect sensibility for a spy. 'Who ran the espionage systems that lived in the ocean of the spirits?' (20), Harry asks himself, alive to the ramifications of the spy as spook – 'how did an agent making copies of secret papers week after week, year after year, keep from himself the awful fear that the spirit sea of misdeeds might seep into the sleep of the man who could catch him?' (20). A professional spook, Hubbard in the Omega chapters is a man haunted – by the ghosts and spirits surrounding his ancestral home, the Keep; by the apparent death of Harlot, his head blown off by a shotgun muzzle pressed against the palate (a suicide like

From Egypt to Langley 137

Hemingway's – not for nothing does Hubbard tell us that Harlot 'had not only been my boss, but my master in the only spiritual art that American men and boys respect – machismo. He gave life courses in grace under pressure' – 15); and haunted in the final Omega chapter by Kittredge's decision to leave their marriage for one of the few men he fears, fellow CIA agent Dix Butler. In the final moments, Hubbard is haunted by the ultimate dread, that of sensing that he is, quite literally, dead:

> The idea that I was still alive was an illusion. The rest of that night had taken place in no larger theatre than the small part of the mind that survives as a guide over the first roads chosen by the dead. . . . If the night had ended with the disappearance of my wife, had it really been my own end that I was mourning? (81)

We are almost back here in the territory and idiom of *Ancient Evenings*, and indeed just as readers of that novel are still awaiting the second book in a never-to-be-completed trilogy which would have told them of Menenhetet's reincarnated destiny, so we may never find out what happens next to Hubbard and Kittredge, and whether Harlot is a ghost or a KGB double-agent. In *Harlot's Ghost* what happens next is that Hubbard goes to ground in the Bronx for a year to write the Omega manuscript, and then flies to Moscow to begin his search for Harlot whom he hopes to find 'here and alive . . . as a most honoured colleague of the KGB' (1122). In his narrow room off the airshaft of the old Hotel Metropole in Moscow he reads the Alpha manuscript, the main body of the novel, in the form of more than 2000 frames of microfilm. This narrative tells of Hubbard's years in the CIA from 1955 to 1965. In his 'Foreword' to this section, Hubbard offers an apologia for what is to come – 'the longest reminiscence ever written by anyone within the Agency':

> This attempt, then, to follow the changes in my character and outlook . . . is not to be read as a memoir. It is rather a *Bildungsroman*, an extended narrative of a young man's education and development. Any sophisticated reader of spy

novels picking up this book in the hope of encountering a splendidly plotted work will discover themselves on unfamiliar ground.... One learns to live with the irony that we who spend our lives in Intelligence usually read spy novels with the wistful sentiment, 'Ah, if only my job could turn out so well-shaped!' (94)

Although Hubbard/Mailer argue that in eschewing the 'well-shaped' (a reference here to traditional spy fiction which has not only ends and beginnings, but also middles) contours of a traditionally plotted spy novel they are giving readers the real thing, a degree of verisimilitude which acts as a corrective to the plot-driven contrivances of tradition, many reviewers and not a few readers will regret the result in the Alpha section of *Harlot's Ghost*. There is considerable irony in the fact that in his creative journalism Mailer should have subjected facts to the transfiguring design we find in, say, *The Armies of the Night*, but that in a work of fiction like *Harlot's Ghost* his readers are expected to do without the well-shaped design in the interests of realism:

> The very good spy novels ... are almost always good because their plots are particularly well put together; they almost always have very little to do with life. The people in them are perfect functionaries toward the needs of the scenario. They don't have a personal life, they have a plot life. You either write a novel which has an emphasis on character or an emphasis on plot, and it's the second that's very well adapted to the spy novel – which has nothing to do, virtually, with life in an Intelligence organisation.[66]

Mailer's decision to write the former of these types of novel, with its emphasis on what Hubbard calls 'the changes in my character and outlook ... a *Bildungsroman*', is an extreme case of the *roman verité*: too little design and too much of the unregenerate minutiae of his experiences in Berlin, in Uruguay, in Florida and Cuba. *Harlot's Ghost* contains some powerful writing and some memorable scenes, but lacks the artifice that would have made it meaningful. In its incomplete condition it is an example of just why the novel (not just the spy novel) as a form has traditionally sought to order and design its subject-matter. It is indeed ironical that Mailer himself in his 'Author's Note' which prefaces the novel argues for the virtues of fiction over fact on the grounds that novelists 'can create superior if imaginative histories out of an enhancement of the real, the unverified, and the wholly fictional' (ix). The main problem with *Harlot's Ghost* is that this 'enhancement of the real' is only occasionally accomplished. Hubbard quotes Thomas Mann's dictum, 'only the exhaustive is truly interesting' in defence of his approach to detail in his narrative, but perhaps to be informed about everything is to know nothing, and too often Hubbard's story gives us information without perspective.

The novel is, in Mailer's description, 'an anti-spy novel', an effort at demythologising the life of the spy. Throughout, there is a good deal of self-conscious appraising of what it means to be an agent of the CIA, though the daily routine is very often far removed from the lofty vision set out in Mailer's essay 'A Harlot High and Low'. Is it, one wonders, Mailer's narrative which declines into inconsequentiality or just his accurate rendition of the inconsequentialities of authentic, demythologised CIA experience? As one critic puts it, 'Hunt's normal agenda is as busy and vacuous as a day in the life of a Jane Austen heroine.' Yet according to Kittredge (a character who sounds very much like her author), such commonplace lives are only disappointing to those who have confused fiction with reality. In one of their many correspondences she tells Hubbard:

> I believe that people like you and me go into intelligence work in the first place because to a much greater degree than we realize, we've been intellectually seduced. And often by nothing more impressive than good spy novels and movies. We want, secretly, to act as protagonists in such ventures. Then we go to work for the Company, and discover that, whatever we are, we are never protagonists . . . the key to our lives, Harry, is in the drear word, *patience*. We are incompetent without it. (533)

Perhaps, wishing to write something a good deal *more* impressive than a 'good spy novel', Mailer in this 'anti-spy novel' asks his readers for a little too much dreary patience.

In one literal sense Kittredge's analysis is all too accurate, for as Eric Homberger remarks in his study of John Le Carré, real-life spies like E. Howard Hunt and Richard Helms could be both consumers and creators of spy fiction:

> Richard Helms . . . admired Fleming's novels. He gave E. Howard Hunt formal permission to write spy thrillers. . . . Before his arrest and imprisonment over the Watergate break-in, Hunt wrote more than forty spy stories under a variety of pseudonyms. The spymaster Allen Dulles firmly believed that the right kind of spy story could strengthen popular support for the Agency. He sometimes passed on suggestions for plots to no doubt grateful thriller writers.[67]

The dreariness of the reality of being a CIA agent was enough, apparently, to explain their imaginative re-creation of heroic protagonists in a spy-world of their own devising. But one is nevertheless faced by the question: if Hunt and other CIA staff would escape from the boring routines of espionage into the melodrama of spy thrillers, why then should Mailer subject his readers to a novel which insists on that boring routine as its untransfigured material? Eric Homberger tells us that 'Sir William Stephenson, wartime head of the British Security Co-ordination agency in North America, advised Ian Fleming, who had worked as his subordinate during the war, that *Casino Royale* couldn't be a success: "It will never sell, Ian. Truth is always less believable".'[68] In *Harlot's Ghost* we receive, unfortunately, an unmediated mass of 'truth'. 'I was trying to create an environment that was life-like in this book', Mailer said, and claimed in his preface to the novel that 'my imaginative CIA is as real or more real than nearly all the lived-in ones' (vii). The problem with this approach is that all too often he allows the documentation of reality to overwhelm the fiction. Although some of the novel's reviewers thought that he had succeeded in his goal of 'imagining' the real CIA, with Anthony Burgess finding that 'we have here a history of the CIA fictionalised out of the zone of bald facts into the realm of the imagination',[69] others put what is, for me, a more persuasive view that 'those who want to read about the real CIA can profitably dip into some of the more than 80 books [Mailer] lists in a bibliography'[70] given at the start of the novel.

It may, then, be enough to judge this novel on its author's stated aim – to give readers an authentic slice of CIA life, and in so doing to demythologise and deconstruct its legend. Yet Mailer told an interviewer that the world of Harlot and Hubbard was one of 'more questions than answers'.[71] Elsewhere he confided that his youthful urge to change the world had become a more objective desire 'to understand' a complex political organism like the CIA.[72] The detachment towards his subject is also shown in his remark that he would be content if 'half the people who read [the novel] say the CIA should be junked, and the other half say they want to join it'.[73] Such comments suggest that his point of view was to be more philosophical than political in kind. As in the previous novel, we encounter in *Harlot's Ghost* a good deal that is familiar in terms of Mailer's philosophical *principia*, with Harlot and Kittredge being the main sources of such wisdom. Kittredge is, literally, the Alpha and Omega in this regard, with her conviction that every psyche is divided into an Alpha and an Omega that are unknown to each other. She is on the CIA staff as a kind of solo think-tank, a psychologist whose research in personality theory is funded, one presumes, for its applications to national as well as individual character. Her ideas are both a reaction to and a product of a Cold War world of geopolitical division and ideological separatism. Although 'wed together like the corporeal lobes of the brain', the Alpha and Omega in us all can easily 'spend their lives in all-out strife for power over the other':

> one of them, Omega, originated in the ovum and so knows more about the mysteries – conception, birth, death, night, the moon, eternity, karma, ghosts, divinities, myths, magic, our primitive past, so on. The other, Alpha, creature of the forward – swimming energies of sperm, ambitious, blind to all but its own purpose, tends, of course, to be more oriented to-

ward enterprise, technology . . . building the bridges between money and power. (433)

The metaphor for humanity in constant struggle with itself does make sense in terms of a postwar psychology, though in the novel Mailer allows the theory to become tediously overused. Almost every one of Kittredge's many letters to Hubbard seems to carry the obligatory reference to the theory until it seems to get up and speak on its own. As one of the novel's major intellectual underpinnings it becomes increasingly feeble, though its macrocosmic applications were sound enough. It is, though, very old Mailer dressed up in new clothes and can be traced back beyond the dualistic psychology sketched out in 'A Harlot High and Low' ('the human brain is divided into a right lobe and a left lobe'), at least as far as the late 1950s and 'Superman Comes to the Supermarket' ('since the First World War Americans have been leading a double life'). The determination to use Alpha/Omega to explain nearly everything, from the psychological distinctions to be drawn between the Kennedy brothers (924) and Fidel Castro (1035), to Hubbard's love–hate relations with his mother (631), is finally trite.

Yet though *Harlot's Ghost* does not satisfy in its architecture or in its capacity to revise and renew our perception of the American history it treats, it is yet a further instance of what Harold Bloom once called 'the paradox that Mailer's importance seems to transcend any of his individual works'.[74] Perhaps he is, as Frank McConnell once suggested, the Kilroy of American letters, a signature of the age, for

> whenever we encounter a self-conscious, irreverent, dangerous American fiction which attempts to reinvent, through its own stylization, a viable idea of human life and fruitful human passion, we must recognize that somewhere in the background, like Kilroy, Mailer was here.[75]

Yet when those individual works are considered it sometimes seems that Mailer has been all too true to his existential conviction that 'the essence of spirit was to choose the thing which did not better one's position but made it more perilous'.⁷⁶ Both *Ancient Evenings* and *Harlot's Ghost* have hardly bettered his position as a novelist of stature, and it may be significant that both were published as first volumes of a larger unity which Mailer was unable to complete in the case of *Ancient Evenings*, while many will doubt they will ever see the 'excluded middle' section of *Harlot's Ghost*.

Once the advocate of violent dissent, committed to bringing about a revolutionary shift in 'the consciousness of our time', Mailer has more recently looked back in envy at the situation of the writer in the Soviet Union. There, he remarked,

> in the worst days, they had Samizdat; people would write things and they'd be mimeographed and read with unholy intensity. It would change their lives. Most American writers have lost the feeling that they could change anyone's life.⁷⁷

His most recent writing seems to reflect this attrition, as a youthful conception of literature as revolution becomes, in his own words, 'transformed to irony'⁷⁸ and *Harlot's Ghost* offers its readers a Cold War CIA with a genial touch. In the mazy crosshatch of early postmodernism, Mailer was once the beneficiary, mixing high tones with low. Now the fiction has more fade-out than definition but much more than enough will remain, of a fulfilled bold talent, to stand in high relief amongst the greatest writing of his generation.

Notes

Chapter 1 Introduction: The Shaping of Personality

1. 'All Bark And No Bite', *Guardian*, 2 June 1992, p. 17.
2. Ibid.
3. William Reel, 'The Bore Buster', *Sunday News*, 1 June 1969, rpt. in P. Manso (ed.), *Running Against the Machine: The Mailer-Breslin Campaign* (New York, 1969) pp. 124–31.
4. Norman Mailer, 'The Metaphysics of the Belly', in *The Presidential Papers* (New York, 1963) p. 284.
5. Richard Gilman, *The Confusion of Realms* (London, 1970) p. 85.
6. R. C. Harrison, in P. Manso (ed.), *Mailer: His Life and Times* (Harmondsworth, Middx., 1986) p. 62.
7. Robert Begiebing, 'Twelfth Round: An Interview with Norman Mailer', in J. M. Lennon (ed.), *Conversations with Norman Mailer* (Jackson, Miss., 1988) p. 317.
8. Christopher Brookeman, *American Culture and Society since 1930* (London, 1984) p. 150.
9. Hilary Mills, *Mailer: A Biography* (Sevenoaks, Kent, 1983) p. 408.
10. Richard Poirier, *Mailer* (London, 1972) p. 156.
11. M. Linenthal, in Manso, *Mailer*, p. 60.
12. Gregory Hemingway, *Papa: A Personal Memoir* (New York, 1976) p. 103.
13. D. L. Kaufmann, 'The Long Happy Life of Norman Mailer', *Modern Fiction Studies*, vol. 17 (1971) 348–49.
14. A. Kazin, *Bright Book of Life: American Novelists and Storytellers from Hemingway to Mailer* (London, 1974) p. 154.
15. G. W. Goethals, in Manso, *Mailer*, p. 68.
16. Begiebing, 'Twelfth Round', pp. 309–10.
17. Roger Ebert, '"Tough Guy" Mailer Shows He Can Dance with the Big Boys', in Begiebing, 'Twelfth Round', p. 357.
18. R. L. Wolf, in Manso, *Mailer*, p. 10.
19. F. S. Mailer, in Manso, *Mailer*, p. 19.

20. Manso, *Mailer*, p. 32.
21. F. S. Mailer, in Manso, *Mailer*, p. 19.
22. A. Epstein, in Manso, *Mailer*, p. 27.
23. Manso, *Mailer*, p. 345.
24. 'Craft and Consciousness: An Interview With Steven Marcus', in M. Lennon (ed.), *Norman Mailer: Pontifications* (Boston, Mass., 1982) p. 18.
25. Manso, *Mailer*, p. 368.
26. A. Kazin, *Bright Book of Life*, p. 157.
27. M. Radin, in Manso, *Mailer*, p. 13.
28. Norman Podhoretz, *Breaking Ranks: A Political Memoir* (London, 1979) p. 362.
29. Manso, *Mailer*, p. 112.
30. Mills, *Mailer*, p. 93.
31. Ibid., p. 44.
32. Begiebing, 'Twelfth Round', p. 315.
33. Mills, *Mailer*, p. 108.
34. Nigel Leigh, *Radical Fictions and the Novels of Norman Mailer* (London, 1990) pp. 6–7.
35. Podhoretz, *Breaking Ranks*, p. 45.
36. Leigh, *Radical Fictions*, p. 30.
37. 'Writers at Work: Interview with Norman Mailer', *Paris Review*, no. 31 (Winter–Spring 1964) 39.
38. *Advertisements for Myself* (London, 1961) p. 90.
39. *Pontifications*, p. 18.
40. Manso, *Mailer*, p. 155.
41. *Advertisements for Myself*, p. 91.
42. Ibid.
43. W. T. Lhamon, Jr, *Deliberate Speed: The Origins of a Cultural Style in the American 1950s* (Washington, DC, 1990) p. xi.
44. Ibid.
45. *Advertisements for Myself*, p. 91.
46. Manso, *Mailer*, p. 158.
47. Ibid., p. 139.
48. Ibid., p. 138.
49. Mills, *Mailer*, p. 120.
50. Bea Mailer, in Mills, *Mailer*, p. 120.
51. Ibid.
52. Manso, *Mailer*, p. 137.
53. Ibid., p. 185.
54. Ibid., p. 187.
55. Ibid., p. 215.
56. Ibid., pp. 211–12.
57. Ibid., p. 218.

58. *Advertisements for Myself*, p. 221.
59. Manso, *Mailer*, p. 216.
60. Manso, *Mailer*, p. 216.
61. *Advertisements for Myself*, p. 61.
62. Manso, *Mailer*, pp. 144–5.
63. *Advertisements for Myself*, p. 210.
64. Ibid.
65. Manso, *Mailer*, p. 211.
66. *Advertisements for Myself*, p. 250.
67. Mills, *Mailer*, p. 161. Hemingway also told Leslie Fiedler that 'I never got [Mailer's] book. The mails in Cuba are terrible.' In Leslie Fiedler, *A Fiedler Reader* (New York, 1977) pp. 160–61. Certainly Hemingway possessed a copy of *The Naked and the Dead*, part of the library in his Cuban residence, Finca Vigía at San Francisco de Paula, near Havana. See Norberto Fuentes, *Ernest Hemingway Rediscovered* (London, 1988) p. 169.
68. *Advertisements for Myself*, p. 235.
69. Mills, *Mailer*, pp. 128–9.
70. Ibid., p. 141.
71. Kazin, *Bright Book of Life*, pp. 150–1.
72. Brookeman, *American Culture*, p. 153.
73. Kazin, *Bright Book of Life*, p. 151.
74. Manso, *Mailer*, pp. 157–8.
75. Podhoretz, *Breaking Ranks*, p. 47.
76. J. Tallmer, in Manso, *Mailer*, p. 225.
77. *Advertisements for Myself*, pp. 244–5.
78. Ibid., p. 250.
79. Ibid., p. 245.
80. Manso, p. 268.
81. Ibid., p. 253.
82. Mills, *Mailer*, p. 177.
83. C. Brossard, in Mills, *Mailer*, pp. 182–3.
84. F. I. Gwaltney, in Mills, *Mailer*, p. 183.
85. J. Feiffer, in Manso, *Mailer*, p. 269.
86. Mills, *Mailer*, p. 185.
87. Manso, *Mailer*, p. 258.
88. Ibid., p. 269.
89. Ibid., p. 260.
90. Mills, *Mailer*, p. 190.
91. Carlos Baker (ed.), *Ernest Hemingway: Selected Letters 1917–1961* (London, 1981) p. 912.
92. Manso, *Mailer*, p. 274.
93. *Advertisements for Myself*, p. 245.

Notes

94. Manso, *Mailer*, pp. 284–5.
95. Ibid., p. 286.
96. Ibid., p. 264.
97. Ibid., p. 268.
98. N. Podhoretz, in Manso, *Mailer*, p. 267.
99. Ibid., p. 282.
100. Ibid., p. 274.
101. *Advertisements for Myself*, p. 244.
102. M. Mowery, in Manso, *Mailer*, p. 295.
103. R. Friedman, in Manso, *Mailer*, p. 296.
104. Ibid., p. 303.
105. Ibid., p. 286.
106. Dr C. Rosenburg, in Mills, *Mailer*, p. 225.
107. Ibid., p. 227.
108. Mills, *Mailer*, p. 231.
109. Ibid., pp. 231–2.
110. Manso, *Mailer*, pp. 317–8.
111. J. Lowe, in Manso, *Mailer*, p. 328.
112. Dr J. Begner, in Manso, *Mailer*, p. 328.
113. Ibid., p. 329.
114. Ibid., p. 335.
115. Mills, *Mailer*, p. 225.
116. Manso, *Mailer*, p. 327.
117. Ibid., p. 331.
118. ibid., p. 328.
119. Ibid., p. 311.
120. Mills, *Mailer*, p. 226.
121. J. Toback, in Mills, *Mailer*, p. 265.
122. Brookeman, *American Culture*, pp. 158, 160.
123. Manso, *Mailer*, p. 305.
124. Ibid., p. 302.
125. Ibid.
126. 'The Existential Hero', in *The Presidential Papers* (New York, 1963) pp. 46–7.
127. Manso, *Mailer*, p. 365.
128. Mills, *Mailer*, p. 239.
129. 'The Fifth Presidential Paper – The Existential Heroine: An Evening with Jackie Kennedy, or, The Wild West of the East', in *The Presidential Papers*, pp. 94–5.
130. Ibid., p. 96.
131. Ibid., p. 98.
132. 'A Prefatory Paper – Heroes and Leaders', in *The Presidential Papers*, p. 6.

133. 'The Eleventh Presidential Paper – Death: Ten Thousand Words a Minute', in *The Presidential Papers*, p. 255.
134. Manso, *Mailer*, p. 407.
135. Mills, *Mailer*, p. 314.
136. 'Part One: Lambs: Introducing Our Argument', in *Cannibals and Christians* (London, 1967) p. 5.
137. Ibid., p. 2.
138. S. Sontag, *Against Interpretation and Other Essays* (London, 1987) p. 224.
139. *Cannibals and Christians*, p. 3.
140. Diana Trilling, in Manso, *Mailer*, p. 465.
141. Ibid., p. 461.
142. Norman Mailer, *The Armies of the Night: History as a Novel / The Novel as History* (London, 1968) p. 216.
143. Ibid., p. 88.
144. Ibid., p. 87.
145. Ibid., p. 188.
146. Manso, *Mailer*, p. 466.
147. *Of a Fire on the Moon* (Boston, Mass., 1969) p. 15.
148. Ibid., p. 51.
149. Ibid., p. 281.
150. Ibid., p. 73.
151. Ibid., p. 99.
152. Ibid., p. 58.
153. Ibid., p. 86.
154. Norman Mailer, *The Prisoner of Sex* (Boston, Mass., 1971) p. 229.
155. *Of a Fire on the Moon*, p. 15.
156. Ibid., p. 132.
157. *The Prisoner of Sex*, p. 31.
158. Ibid., p. 16.
159. Ibid., p. 233.
160. Manso, *Mailer*, p. 556.
161. Mills, *Mailer*, p. 132.
162. Manso, *Mailer*, p. 132.
163. Ibid., p. 133.
164. Graham McCann, *Marilyn Monroe: The Body in the Library* (Cambridge, 1988) p. 10.
165. *Marilyn: A Biography* (New York, 1973) p. 20.
166. McCann, *Marilyn Monroe*, p. 37.
167. 'I Want to Go Ahead and Do It', *New York Times Book Review*, 7 October 1979, 26.
168. Tim O'Brien, in Manso, *Mailer*, p. 606.
169. Mills, *Mailer*, p. 427.
170. Ibid., p. 14.

Notes 149

171. Manso, *Mailer*, p. 621.
172. Ibid., p. 646.
173. 'Mailer Meets Madonna', *Esquire* (September 1994) 59.
174. Sontag, *Against Interpretation*, p. 49.

Chapter 2 The Hot Breath of the Future: *The Naked and the Dead*

1. *Bright Book of Life*, p. 71.
2. *The Naked and the Dead*, (London, 1949) p. 313.
3. D. Trilling, 'The Moral Radicalism of Norman Mailer', in R. Lucid (ed.), *Norman Mailer: The Man and his Work* (Boston, Mass., 1971) p. 116.
4. 'The Ninth Presidential Paper – Totalitarianism', in *The Presidential Papers*, p. 183.
5. Quoted by Randall H. Waldron, 'The Naked, the Dead and the Machine', in H. Bloom (ed.) *Modern Critical Views: Norman Mailer* (New York, 1986) p. 118.
6. Jean Radford, *Norman Mailer: A Critical Study* (London, 1975) p. 345.
7. P. Manso, *Mailer: His Life and Times* (Harmondsworth, Middx., 1986) p. 101.
8. Marvin Mudrick, 'Mailer and Styron: Guests of the Establishment', *Hudson Review*, vol. 17 (1964) 353.
9. N. Leigh, *Radical Fictions and the Novels of Norman Mailer* (Houndmills, Hampshire, 1990) p. 7.
10. *Dangling Man* (London, 1946) pp. 190–1.
11. Ibid., p. 191.
12. R. Poirier, *Mailer*, (London, 1972) p. 28.
13. Leigh, *Radical Fictions*, p. 7.
14. Waldron, 'The Naked, the Dead and the Machine', p. 118.
15. Ibid., p. 119.
16. Ibid., p. 125.
17. Leigh, *Radical Fictions* p. 21.
18. R. Solotaroff, *Down Mailer's Way* (Urbana, Ill., 1974) pp. 30, 38.
19. R. Gilman, 'Norman Mailer: Art as Life, Life as Art', in his *The Confusion of Realms* (London, 1970) p. 98.
20. *The Presidential Papers*, p. 84.
21. Radford, *Norman Mailer*, p. 48.
22. J. Wenke, *Mailer's America* (Hanover, NH, 1987) pp. 9–10.
23. In Manso, *Mailer*, p. 397.
24. 'The Third Presidential Paper – The Existential Hero: Superman Comes to the Supermarket', in *The Presidential Papers*, p. 38.
25. Solotaroff, *Down Mailer's Way* p. 27.
26. Leigh, *Radical Fictions*, p. 26.
27. Poirier, *Mailer*, p. 33.
28. Wenke, *Mailer's America*, p. 9.

29. Ibid., p. 8.
30. Manso, *Mailer*, p. 101.
31. A. Adams, in Manso, *Mailer*, p. 114.
32. M. Linenthal, in Manso, *Mailer*, p. 114.
33. Ibid.
34. Manso, *Mailer*, p. 101.
35. Leigh, *Radical Fictions*, p. 15.
36. Ibid., p. 13.
37. L. Fiedler, *Love and Death in the American Novel* (London, 1970) p. 406.
38. R. Merrill, *Norman Mailer* (Boston, Mass., 1975) p. 38.
39. Leigh, *Radical Fictions*, p. 15.
40. Ibid., p. 20.
41. N. Podhoretz, 'Norman Mailer: The Embattled Vision', in *Norman Mailer: The Man and his Work*, pp. 67–8.

Chapter 3 Ambush in the Alley: *Barbary Shore* and *The Deer Park*

1. R. Merrill, *Norman Mailer* (Boston, Mass., 1978) p. 43.
2. 'Second Advertisement for Myself: *Barbary Shore*', in *Advertisements for Myself*, p. 91.
3. Merrill, *Norman Mailer*, p. 43.
4. R. Gilman, 'Norman Mailer: Art as Life, Life as Art', in *The Confusion of Realms* (London, 1970) p. 100.
5. Louis Harap, *In the Mainstream: The Jewish Presence in Twentieth-century American Literature, 1950s–1980s* (New York, 1987) p. 153.
6. Robert Alter, 'Norman Mailer', in G. A. Panichas (ed.), *The Politics of Twentieth-century Novelists* (New York, 1976) p. 321.
7. R. Solotaroff, *Down Mailer's Way* (Urbana, Ill., 1974) p. 52n.
8. M. Mudrick, 'Mailer and Styron: Guests of the Establishment', *Hudson Review*, vol. 17 (1964) p. 353.
9. Quoted in Jean Radford, *Norman Mailer: A Critical Study* (London, 1974) p. 84.
10. R. Poirier, *Mailer* (London, 1972) p. 71.
11. Solotaroff, *Down Mailer's Way* p. 226.
12. 'Second Advertisement for Myself', pp. 91–2.
13. Ibid., p. 103.
14. Ibid., p. 91.
15. 'Third Advertisement for Myself', in *Advertisements for Myself*, p. 103.
16. N. Leigh, *Radical Fictions and the Novels of Norman Mailer* (Houndmills, Hampshire, 1990) p. 37.
17. John Stark, '*Barbary Shore*: The Basis of Mailer's Best Work', *Modern Fiction Studies*, vol. 17 (1971) 406.
18. D. Trilling, 'The Moral Radicalism of Norman Mailer', in R. F. Lucid (ed.), *Norman Mailer: The Man and his Work* (Boston, Mass., 1971) p. 119.

19. Robert Ehrlich, *Norman Mailer: The Radical as Hipster* (Metuchen, NJ, 1978) p. 36.
20. Stark, *'Barbary Shore'*, p. 405.
21. 'Third Advertisement for Myself', p. 103.
22. Poirier, *Mailer*, p. 76.
23. Stark, *'Barbary Shore'*, p. 405.
24. Radford, *Norman Mailer*, p. 16.
25. Leigh, *Radical Fictions*, p. 36.
26. P. Bufithis, *Norman Mailer* (New York, 1978) p. 33.
27. Ibid.
28. 'Second Advertisement for Myself: *Barbary Shore*', p. 91.
29. Ibid.
30. *The Deer Park* (New York, 1955).
31. 'Fourth Advertisement for Myself': The Last Draft of *The Deer Park*, in *Advertisements for Myself*, p. 11.
32. See Michael Millgate, *American Social Fiction: James to Cozzens* (Edinburgh, 1964) pp. 159–62.
33. M. F. Schulz, 'Norman Mailer's Divine Comedy', in his *Radical Sophistication: Studies in Contemporary Jewish-American Novelists* (Athens, Ohio, 1969) p. 84.
34. P. B. Shelley, *Selected Poems*, ed. Timothy Webb (London, 1977) p. 11.
35. *Cannibals and Christians*, pp. 186–7.
36. Ibid., p. 182.
37. Ibid.
38. Poirier, *Mailer*, p. 12.
39. *Cannibals and Christians*, p. 183.
40. Ibid.
41. R. Lowell, 'For the Union Dead', in *Life Studies and For the Union Dead* (New York, 1971) p. 70.
42. D. L. Kaufmann, *Norman Mailer: The Countdown (The First Twenty Years)* (Carbondale, Ill., 1969) p. 25.
43. G. Steiner, 'Naked but not Dead', in J. Michael Lennon (ed.), *Critical Essays on Norman Mailer* (Boston, Mass., 1986) p. 53.
44. Poirier, *Mailer*, p. 37.
45. W. J. Weatherby, *Conversations with Marilyn* (London, 1976) p. 143.
46. 'Fourth Advertisement for Myself', p. 211.
47. R. Foster, *Norman Mailer* (Minneapolis, Minn., 1968) p. 16.
48. Mudrick, 'Mailer and Styron', p. 358.
49. Kaufmann, *Norman Mailer* pp. 26–7.
50. Mudrick, 'Mailer and Styron', p. 355.
51. B. Gill, 'Small Trumpet', in *Critical Essays on Norman Mailer*, p. 47.
52. See Merrill, *Norman Mailer*, p. 44.
53. Gill, 'Small Trumpet', p. 48.
54. Leigh, *Radical Fictions*, pp. 61–2.

55. F. D. McConnell, *Four Postwar American Novelists: Bellow, Mailer, Barth, and Pynchon* (Chicago, Ill., 1977) p. 91.
56. In his *Existential Errands* (Boston, Mass., 1972) p. 267, Mailer attributes this line to D. H. Lawrence.
57. McConnell, *Four Postwar American Novelists*, p. 89.
58. S. T. Gutman, *Mankind in Barbary: The Individual and Society in the Novels of Norman Mailer* (Hanover, NH, 1975) p. 60.
59. Ibid.
60. Gilman, 'Norman Mailer', p. 102.
61. Poirier, *Mailer*, p. 37.
62. Bufithis, *Norman Mailer*, p. 49.
63. 'Fourth Advertisement for Myself', p.206.
64. L. Adams, *Existential Battles: The Growth of Norman Mailer* (Athens, Ohio, 1976) p. 49.
65. Merrill, *Norman Mailer*, p. 44.
66. 'Introduction' in H. Bloom (ed.), *Modern Critical Views: Norman Mailer* (New York, 1986) p. 3.
67. Mudrick, 'Mailer and Styron', p. 351.
68. Leigh, *Radical Fictions*, p. 81.
69. Trilling, 'Moral Radicalism', p. 126.
70. Norman Mailer, 'The White Negro: Superficial Reflections on the Hipster', in *Advertisements for Myself*, pp. 295–6.
71. Leigh, *Radical Fictions* p. 80.
72. Trilling, 'Moral Radicalism', p. 126.

Chapter 4 A Plunge into the Age: *An American Dream* and *Why Are We in Vietnam?*

1. P. Manso, *Mailer: His Life and Times* (Harmondsworth, Middx., 1986) pp. 384–8.
2. Ibid., p. 386.
3. A. Kazin, 'The Decline of War: Mailer to Vonnegut', in *Bright Book of Life: American Novelists and Storytellers from Hemingway to Mailer* (New York 1974) p. 154.
4. 'First Advertisement for Myself', in *Advertisements for Myself*, p. 17.
5. H. Mills, *Mailer: A Biography* (Sevenoaks, Kent, 1983) p. 408.
6. J. Radford, *Norman Mailer: A Critical Study* (London, 1975) p. 155.
7. E. Hardwick, 'Bad Boy', *Partisan Review*, vol. 32 (1965) 292.
8. M. Mudrick, 'Mailer and Styron: Guests of the Establishment', *Hudson Review*, vol. 17 (1964) p. 363n.
9. M. Amis, *The Moronic Inferno and Other Visits to America* (London, 1986) p. 63.
10. Manso, *Mailer*, p. 403.
11. Ibid.

Notes

12. R. Poirier, 'Morbid-Mindedness', in R. F. Lucid (ed.), *Norman Mailer: The Man and his Work*, p. 163.
13. *An American Dream* (London, 1965) p. 9.
14. F. D. McConnell, 'Norman Mailer and the Cutting Edge of Style', in *Four Postwar American Novelists: Bellow, Mailer, Barth and Pynchon* (Chicago, Ill., 1977) pp. 95–6.
15. 'In the Red Light: A History of the Republican Convention in 1964', in *Cannibals and Christians*, p. 7.
16. *Cannibals and Christians*, p. 143.
17. Leo Bersani, 'The Interpretation of Dreams', in R. F. Lucid (ed.), *Norman Mailer: The Man and his Work*, p. 173.
18. *Cannibals and Christians*, pp. 42–3.
19. 'A Speech at Berkeley on Vietnam Day', in *Cannibals and Christians*, p. 74.
20. *Cannibals and Christians*, p. 42.
21. 'How the Wimp Won the War', *Vanity Fair* (May 1991) p. 70.
22. Ibid., p. 71.
23. Ibid.
24. Personal interview, 21 October 1991.
25. Ibid.
26. 'The Leading Man: A Review of *J.F.K.: The Man and The Myth*', in *Cannibals and Christians*, pp. 141–2.
27. Ibid., p. 142.
28. *Cannibals and Christians*, pp. 53–4.
29. Don DeLillo, *Libra* (London, 1989) p. 181.
30. Ibid., p. 15.
31. L. Adams, *Existential Battles: The Growth of Norman Mailer* (Athens, Ohio, 1976) p. 71.
32. M. F. Schulz, 'Norman Mailer's Divine Comedy', in *Radical Sophistication: Studies in Contemporary Jewish-American Novelists* (Athens, Ohio, 1969) p. 96.
33. McConnell, 'Norman Mailer', p. 98.
34. J. Wenke, *Mailer's America* (Hanover, NH, 1987) p. 99.
35. Poirier, 'Morbid-Mindedness', p. 165.
36. DeLillo, *Libra*, p. 456.
37. L. Fiedler, 'The Jew in a Gentile World', in *The Fiedler Reader* (New York, 1977) p. 236.
38. 'Footfalls in the Crypt', *Vanity Fair* (February 1992) 81.
39. *Deaths for the Ladies (And Other Disasters)* (1962), *The Bullfight: A Photographic Narrative with Text By Norman Mailer* (1967), *The Deer Park: A Play* (1967), *Miami and the Siege of Chicago* (1968), *The Armies of the Night* (1968) and *Of a Fire on the Moon* (1970). In addition, Mailer produced three films, *Wild 90* (1967), *Beyond the Law* (1968) and *Maidstone* (1970).
40. *The Norton Anthology of Poetry*, 3rd edn (New York, 1983) p. 794.
41. This was due to the paper going out of business.

42. P. Beidler, *Re-writing America: Vietnam Authors in their Generation* (Athens, Ga., 1991) pp. 208, 312 n. 4.
43. J. M. Lennon (ed.), *Conversations with Norman Mailer*, (Jackson, Miss., 1988) p. 114.
44. Wenke, *Mailer's America*, pp. 122–3.
45. McConnell, 'Norman Mailer', p. 101.
46. Stacey Olster, *Reminiscence and Re-creation in Contemporary American Fiction* (Cambridge, 1989) p. 46.
47. *Why Are We in Vietnam? A Novel* (London, 1969).
48. L. Adams, *Existential Battles*, p. 115.
49. Wenke, *Mailer's America*, p. 128.
50. P. Bufithis, *Norman Mailer* (New York, 1978) p. 76.
51. R. Solotaroff, *Down Mailer's Way* (Urbana, Ill., 1974) p. 195.
52. *The Armies of the Night*, p. 48.
53. Ibid., p. 49.
54. Ibid., p. 48.
55. Beidler, *Re-writing America*, p. 208.
56. I. Hassan, *Selves at Risk: Patterns of Quest in Contemporary American Letters* (Madison, Wis., 1990) p. 124.
57. Poirier, *Mailer*, p. 153.
58. 'The Argument Reinvigorated', *Cannibals and Christians*, p. 95.
59. *Cannibals and Christians*, p. 85.
60. *The Armies of the Night*, p. 189.
61. *Cannibals and Christians*, p. 110.
62. Solotaroff, *Down Mailer's Way*, p. 203.
63. *Cannibals and Christians*, p. 110.
64. J. W. Aldridge, 'From Vietnam to Obscenity', in R. F. Lucid (ed.), *Norman Mailer: The Man and his Work*, p. 184.
65. At least two critics acknowledge this ironic reading. See J. Aldridge, 'From Vietnam to Obscenity', pp. 191–2, and R. Ramsey, 'Current and Recurrent: The Vietnam Novel', *Modern Fiction Studies*, vol. 17 (1971) 419.
66. B. H. Leeds, *The Structured Vision of Norman Mailer* (New York, 1969) p. 201.
67. Richard Godden, *Fictions of Capital: The American Novel from James to Mailer* (Cambridge, 1990) p. 189.
68. Edward Jay Epstein, *Inquest: The Warren Commission and the Establishment of Truth* (London, 1966) p. 72.
69. Laura Adams, 'Existential Aesthetics: An Interview with Norman Mailer', in J. M. Lennon (ed.), *Conversations with Norman Mailer*, p. 213.
70. Ibid., p. 212.
71. Ibid., pp. 212–13.
72. M. Herr, *Dispatches* (London, 1978) p. 42.

Notes 155

Chapter 5 From Egypt to Langley: *Ancient Evenings, Tough Guys Don't Dance* **and** *Harlot's Ghost*

1. *The Armies of the Night*, pp. 21–2.
2. P. Manso, *Mailer: His Life and Times* (Harmondsworth, Middx., 1986) p. 665.
3. 'Last Advertisement for Myself Before the Way Out', in *Advertisements for Myself*, p. 412.
4. In J. M. Lennon (ed.), *Conversations with Norman Mailer* (Jackson, Miss., 1988) p. 368. See also his interview with M. Lennon, 'Literary Ambitions,' in *Pontifications*, pp. 170–71, where he discusses his plans for the trilogy.
5. Interview with Melvyn Bragg, 'Mailer Takes on the Pharaohs', *The Sunday Times Magazine*, 5 June 1983, p. 19.
6. Manso, *Mailer*, p. 658.
7. Wenke and Leigh include chapters on the novel, as does Robert Begiebing, in his *Toward a New Synthesis: John Fowles, John Gardner, Norman Mailer* (Ann Arbor, Mich., 1989) pp. 87–125.
8. N. Leigh, *Radical Fictions and the Novels of Norman Mailer* p. 149.
9. Barry H. Leeds, 'A Conversation with Norman Mailer', in Lennon, *Conversations with Norman Mailer*, p. 369.
10. Walter Clemons, *Vanity Fair*, quoted in Manso, *Mailer*, p. 657.
11. Ibid., p. 656.
12. R. Poirier, 'In Pyramid and Palace', in Lennon, *Critical Essays on Norman Mailer*, p. 83.
13. Lennon, *Conversations with Norman Mailer*, p. 299.
14. 'Norman in Egypt: "Ancient Evenings"', in H. Bloom (ed.), *Norman Mailer* (New York, 1986) p. 200.
15. Clemons, *Vanity Fair*, p. 657.
16. Norman Mailer, *Ancient Evenings* (Boston, Mass., 1983) pp. 112–14.
17. Lennon, *Conversations with Norman Mailer*, p. 300.
18. Personal letter, 10 December 1993.
19. P. Brooks, 'The Melodramatic Imagination', *Partisan Review*, vol. 2 (1972) 204.
20. Ibid., pp. 209–10.
21. *Fictions of Capital*, pp. 214–15.
22. *The Fight* (Boston, Mass., 1975) pp. 72–3.
23. *Cannibals and Christians*, p. 42.
24. Norman Mailer, *The Executioner's Song* (Boston, Mass., 1979) p. 692.
25. *The Presidential Papers*, p. 214.
26. Poirier, 'In Pyramid and Palace', p. 86.
27. *The Presidential Papers*, p. 95.
28. James Wolcott, 'Happy Man Haunted by Papa', *Observer*, 13 October 1991, p. 59.

29. Lennon, *Conversations with Norman Mailer*, p. 365.
30. Manso, *Mailer*, p. 663.
31. Michael Ventura, 'Dance of a Tough Guy', in Lennon, *Conversations with Norman Mailer*, p. 380.
32. Lennon, *Conversations with Norman Mailer*, p. 365.
33. Interview with C. Bigsby, BBC Radio 3, 'Third Ear', 12 November 1991.
34. Ibid.
35. Ventura, 'Dance of a Tough Guy', p. 308.
36. Wilfrid Sheed, 'Armageddon Now?', *New York Review of Books*, 5 December 1991, p. 41.
37. Ibid.
38. Manso, *Mailer*, p. 664.
39. *Tough Guys Don't Dance* (New York, 1984) p. 228.
40. *Some Honorable Men: Political Conventions 1960–1972* (Boston, Mass., 1976) p. x.
41. Personal Interview, 21 October 1991.
42. *The Armies of the Night*, p. 124.
43. Interview with Peter Stothard, 'Soft Spots in a Tough Guise', *The Times Saturday Review*, 12 October 1991, p. 16.
44. Paul Gray, 'Harlot's Ghost: A Ghastly Tale', *Time*, 30 September 1991, p. 70.
45. Scott Spencer, 'The Old Man and the Novel', *Guardian*, 5 October 1991, p. 20.
46. Wolcott, 'Happy Man', p. 59.
47. Peter Kemp, 'The Incredible Bulk', *The Sunday Times Review*, 20 October 1991, Section 7, p. 2.
48. Gray, 'Harlot's Ghost', p. 70.
49. John Sutherland, 'The Paranoia Factory', *The Times Literary Supplement*, 18 October 1991, p. 20.
50. Robert Wilson, 'Mailer's Creative Intelligence is Central to "Harlot's Ghost"', *USA Today*, 27 September 1991, p. 5D.
51. A. Burgess, 'A Short History of Our Time', *Washington Post Book World*, 29 September 1991, p. 1.
52. Ibid., p. 10.
53. Spencer, 'The Old Man and the Novel', p. 21.
54. Personal letter, 10 December 1993.
55. 'A Harlot High and Low', in *Pieces and Pontifications* (Boston, Mass., 1982) p. 159.
56. Spencer, 'The Old Man and the Novel', p. 21.
57. 'A Harlot High and Low', p. 161.
58. Ibid., p. 162.
59. Ibid., pp. 165–6.
60. Ibid., p. 166.
61. Burgess, 'Short History', p. 10.

62. Interview with Christopher Bigsby, BBC Radio 3, *Third Ear*, 12 November 1991.
63. Sheed, 'Armageddon Now?', p. 48.
64. Ibid., p. 47.
65. Gray, 'Harlot's Ghost', p. 70.
66. Personal interview, 21 October 1991.
67. E. Homberger, *John Le Carré* (London, 1986) p. 26.
68. Ibid.
69. Burgess, 'Short History', p. 10.
70. Gray, 'Harlot's Ghost', p. 70.
71. 'Life's Like That', *Economist*, 26 October 1991, p. 154.
72. Stothard, 'Soft Spots', p. 16.
73. Spencer, 'The Old Man and the Novel', p. 22.
74. 'Introduction', in H. Bloom (ed.), *Norman Mailer*, p. 4.
75. F. D. McConnell, 'Norman Mailer and the Cutting Edge of Style', p. 107.
76. *The Deer Park*, p. 346. See also his 'Two Oddments from *Esquire*', in *The Existential Papers*, p. 267.
77. Interview with Martin Amis, *The Late Show*, BBC TV, 23 October 1991.
78. Norman Mailer, in Stothard, 'Soft Spots', p. 17.

Select Bibliography

WORKS BY MAILER

(Page references in the text are to the following editions)
The Naked and the Dead (London, 1949).
Barbary Shore (New York, 1963).
The Deer Park (New York, 1955)
Advertisements for Myself (London, 1961).
The Presidential Papers (New York, 1963).
An American Dream (London, 1965).
Cannibals and Christians (London, 1967).
Why Are We in Vietnam? (London, 1969).
The Armies of the Night (London, 1968).
Miami and the Siege of Chicago (London, 1968).
Of a Fire on the Moon (Boston, 1970).
The Prisoner of Sex (Boston, 1971).
Existential Errands (Boston, 1971).
Marilyn: A Biography (New York, 1973).
The Fight (Boston, 1975).
Some Honorable Men: Political Conventions 1960–1972 (Boston, 1976).
The Executioner's Song (Boston, 1979).
Ancient Evenings (Boston, 1983).
Tough Guys Don't Dance (New York, 1984).
Harlot's Ghost (London, 1991).

CRITICAL MATERIAL

Books

★ Adams, Laura, *Existential Battles: The Growth of Norman Mailer* (Athens, Ohio, 1976).

Select Bibliography

Adams, Laura (ed.), *Will the Real Norman Mailer Please Stand Up?* (Port Washington, NY, 1974).
Bailey, Jennifer, *Norman Mailer: Quick-Change Artist* (London, 1979).
Begiebing, Robert, *Acts of Regeneration: Allegory and Archetype in the Works of Norman Mailer* (Columbia, 1980).
Begiebing, Robert, *Toward a New Synthesis: John Fowles, John Gardner, Norman Mailer* (Ann Arbor, Michigan, 1989).
* Bloom, Harold (ed.), *Modern Critical Views: Norman Mailer* (New York, 1986).
* Braudy, Leo, *Norman Mailer: A Collection of Critical Essays* (Englewood Cliffs, NJ, 1972).
Bufithis, Philip, *Norman Mailer* (New York, 1978).
Ehrlich, Robert, *Norman Mailer: The Radical as Hipster* (Metuchen, NJ, 1978).
Flaherty, Joe, *Managing Mailer* (New York, 1971).
Foster, Richard, *Norman Mailer* (Minneapolis, 1968).
* Gordon, Andrew, *An American Dreamer: A Psychoanalytic Study of the Fiction of Norman Mailer* (Toronto, 1980).
Gutman, Stanley T., *Mankind in Barbary: The Individual and Society in the Novels of Norman Mailer* (Hanover, NH, 1975).
* Kaufmann, Donald L., *Norman Mailer: The Countdown (The First Twenty Years)* (Carbondale, Ill., 1969).
Leeds, Barry H., *The Structured Vision of Norman Mailer* (New York, 1969).
Leigh, Nigel, *Radical Fictions and the Novels of Norman Mailer* (Basingstoke, Hampshire, 1990).
* Lennon, J. Michael (ed.), *Critical Essays on Norman Mailer* (Boston, 1986).
Lennon, J. Michael (ed.), *Conversations with Norman Mailer* (Jackson, Miss., 1988).
Lucid, Robert F. (ed.), *Norman Mailer: The Man and his Work* (Boston, Mass., 1971).
Manso, Peter, *Mailer: His Life and Times* (Harmondsworth, Middx., 1986).
Manso, Peter (ed.), *Running Against the Machine: The Mailer-Breslin Campaign* (New York, 1969).
Merrill, Robert, *Norman Mailer* (Boston, Mass., 1978).
Mills, Hilary, *Mailer: A Biography* (Sevenoaks, Kent, 1983).
Poirier, Richard, *Mailer* (London, 1972).
Radford, Jean, *Norman Mailer: A Critical Study* (London, 1975).
Solotaroff, Robert, *Down Mailer's Way* (Urbana, Ill., 1974).
Weatherby, W. J., *Squaring Off: Mailer V. Baldwin* (London, 1977).
Wenke, Joseph, *Mailer's America* (Hanover, NH, 1987).

Articles and essays

Aldridge, John W., 'From Vietnam to Obscenity', in R. F. Lucid (ed.), *Norman Mailer: The Man and his Work* (Boston, Mass., 1971) pp. 180–192.

Select Bibliography

Alter, Robert, 'Norman Mailer', in G. A. Panichas (ed.), *The Politics of Twentieth-century Novelists* (New York, 1974) pp. 321–6.

Amis, Martin, 'Norman Mailer: The Avenger and the Bitch', in his *The Moronic Inferno and Other Visits to America* (London, 1986) pp. 57–73.

Baldwin, James, 'The Black Boy Looks at the White Boy', in his *Nobody Knows my Name: More Notes of a Native Son* (London, 1964) pp. 177–96.

Bersani, Leo, 'The Interpretation of Dreams', *Partisan Review*, vol. 32 (1965) 603–8.

Bloom, Harold, 'Norman in Egypt: *Ancient Evenings*', in H. Bloom (ed.), *Modern Critical Views: Norman Mailer* (New York, 1986) pp. 193–200.

Bragg, Melvyn, 'Mailer Takes on the Pharaohs', *Sunday Times Magazine*, 5 June 1983, 18–19.

Brookeman, Christopher, 'Norman Mailer and Mass America', in his *American Culture and Society since the 1930s* (London, 1984) pp. 150–70.

Finholt, Richard D., '"Otherwise How Explain?" Norman Mailer's New Cosmology', *Modern Fiction Studies*, vol. 17 (1971) 375–86.

Gilman, Richard, 'Norman Mailer: Art as Life, Life as Art', in his *The Confusion of Realms* (London, 1970) pp. 81–153.

Godden, Richard, *Fictions of Capital: The American Novel from James to Mailer* (Cambridge, 1990) ch. 7–9, pp. 183–250.

Harap, Louis, 'The Jew Manqué: Norman Mailer', in his *In the Mainstream: The Jewish Presence in Twentieth-century American Literature, 1950s–1980s* (New York, 1987) pp. 151–160.

Hardwick, Elizabeth, 'Bad Boy', *Partisan Review*, vol. 32 (1965) 291–4.

Hassan, Ihab, *Selves at Risk: Patterns of Quest in Contemporary American Letters* (Madison, Wis., 1990).

Kaufmann, Donald L., 'The Long Happy Life of Norman Mailer', *Modern Fiction Studies*, vol. 17 (1971) 347–59.

Kazin, Alfred, 'The Decline of War: Mailer to Vonnegut', in his *Bright Book of Life: American Novelists and Storytellers from Hemingway to Mailer* (New York, 1974) pp. 69–74.

Langbaum, Robert, 'Mailer's New Style', *Novel*, vol. 2 (Fall 1968) 69–78.

Lodge, David, 'Mailer and Female', in his *Write On: Occasional Essays, 1965–1985* (London, 1988) pp. 88–91.

McConnell, Frank D., 'Norman Mailer and the Cutting Edge of Style', in his *Four Postwar American Novelists: Bellow, Mailer, Barth and Pynchon* (Chicago, 1977) pp. 58–107.

Mudrick, Marvin, 'Mailer and Styron: Guests of the Establishment', *Hudson Review*, vol. 17 (1964) 346–66.

Olster, Stacey, 'Norman Mailer: A New Frontier in Fiction', in her *Reminiscence and Re-creation in Contemporary American Fiction* (Cambridge, 1989) pp. 36–71.

Select Bibliography

Pearce, Richard, 'Norman Mailer's *Why Are We in Vietnam?*: A Radical Critique of Frontier Values', *Modern Fiction Studies*, vol. 17 (1971) 409–14.

Podhoretz, Norman, 'Norman Mailer: The Embattled Vision', *Partisan Review*, vol. 26 (1959) 371–91. Reprinted in Lucid (1971) pp. 60–85.

Poirier, Richard, 'Morbid-Mindedness', in Lucid (1971) pp. 162–170.

Ramsey, Roger, 'Current and Recurrent: The Vietnam Novel', *Modern Fiction Studies*, vol. 17 (1971) 415–31.

Richardson, Jack, 'The Aesthetics of Norman Mailer', *New York Review of Books*, 7 May 1969, 2–4.

Ricks, Christopher, 'Mailer's Primal Words', *Grand Street*, vol. 3 (1983) 161–72.

Schulz, Max F., 'Norman Mailer's Divine Comedy' in his *Radical Sophistication: Studies in Contemporary Jewish-American Novelists* (Athens, Ohio, 1969) pp. 69–109.

Scott, Nathan A., Jr, 'Norman Mailer – Our Whitman', in his *Three American Moralists: Mailer, Bellow, Trilling* (Notre Dame, Ind., 1973) pp. 13–98.

Sheed, Wilfrid, 'Armageddon Now?' *New York Review of Books*, 5 December 1991, 41–8.

Stark, John, '*Barbary Shore*: The Basis of Mailer's Best Work', *Modern Fiction Studies*, vol. 17 (1971) 403–8.

Tanner, Tony, 'On the Parapet: A Study of the Novels of Norman Mailer', *Critical Quarterly*, vol. 12 (1970) 153–76. Reprinted in his *City of Words: American Fiction 1950–1970* (London, 1971) pp. 344–71.

Trilling, Diana, 'The Moral Radicalism of Norman Mailer', in Lucid (1971) pp. 108–36.

Vidal, Gore, 'The Angels Are White', in H. Bloom (1986) pp. 7–16.

Waldron, Randall H., 'The Naked, the Dead, and the Machine', in H. Bloom (1986) pp. 115–26.

Index

Advertisements for Myself 13, 15, 23–25, 63–4, 65, 68, 82, **84–100**, 101, 126
American Dream, An 6, 15, 28, 35, 53, 68, 82, **84–100**, 101, 126
   allusions to President John F. Kennedy in 89–99
   critical views of 86–9, 94, 96–8
   serialisation of 84, 86
   style of 84–6
Ancient Evenings 43–4, 73, 100, **115–26**, 137, 143
   composition of 115–16
   reviews of 116–19
   mysticism in 120–2
Armies of the Night, The 28, 35, 36, 39, 42, 100, 103, 106
Arnold, Matthew 100

Balzac, H. de 132, 133
Barbary Shore 6, 53, **62–71**, 72, 78
   autobiographical roots of 63–5, 68
   critical views of 62–3, 67, 69, 71
   politics of 6–9, 53, 67–8, 70, 71
Beat movement 24–5
Bellow, Saul 49
Breslin, Jimmy 39
Burroughs, William, *Naked Lunch* 106, 109

Campbell, Lady Jeanne 5, 33
Cannibals and Christians 35, 36, 73–4, 90, 92, 101, 104–5, 107
Capote, Truman 42
Church, Barbara Norris 42

Deer Park, The 13–19, 32, **72–83**
   critical views of 76–81
DeLillo, Don, *Libra* 95–6, 98

Executioner's Song, The 41–2, 43, 124

Faulkner, William 113
Fitzgerald, F. Scott 22, 88
   The Great Gatsby 72–3, 77–8
Fleming, Ian 140

Ginsberg, Allen 21–2, 24–5

Harlot's Ghost 43–4, 64, **130–43**
   CIA in 130–43
   genre of 131–2, 139
   narrative structure of 135–8
   origins of 133–4
   reviews of 132, 135, 136, 140–1
   themes of 133–5
Hemingway, Ernest 1, 2–3, 22, 23, 90
Herr, Michael, *Dispatches* 104, 113

Index

Hipster, the 20, 24–5, 64, 80, 82–3

Johnson, President Lyndon B. 35, 110–11

Keats, John, 'La Belle Dame Sans Merci' 69
Kennedy, Jacqueline Bouvier 33
Kennedy, President John F. 28, 31–3, 88–99, 102, 107, 110–11
Kerouac, Jack 16, 21, 24–5, 41

Lowell, Robert, 88, 115
'For the Union Dead' 75–6

Mailer, Isaac Barnett 'Barney' (father) 4, 11–12
Mailer, Fanny Schneider (mother) 4–5, 29
Mailer, Norman
  education of 2, 3, 4–5, 7
  existentialist philosophy of 111, 124
  Hollywood and 8, 10–13
  Jewishness of 2, 4, 5, 59–60
  marriage relationships of 5, 10–11, 13, 20–1, 27–30, 33
  New Journalism and 32, 36, 42
  politics of 1, 6–9, 11–12, 18–19, 25, 34–5, 38–9, 74, 93, 103, 110
  postmodernism of 107–8
  theology of 110–11
  totalitarianism and 17, 46–7, 73–4, 76, 92
  violence and 14, 15, 16, 20–1, 25–31, 52
  works *see under individual titles*
Malaquais, Jean 7–8, 9
Marilyn 13, 40–1, 117

Miami and the Siege of Chicago 6, 28, 35
Monroe, Marilyn 40–1, 77, 90, 117

Of a Fire on the Moon 35, 38–9

Presidential Papers, The 34, 47, 52–3, 73, 85, 124
Prisoner of Sex, The 115

Rubin, Jerry 35, 36

Shelley, Percy Bysshe,
  'Ozymandias' 73
Silverman, Beatrice 7, 10–11, 15–16
Sontag, Susan 36, 45
'Superman Comes to the Supermarket' 31, 56–7

Thoreau, Henry D. 113
Tough Guys Don't Dance 126–9
Trilling, Diana 23–4
Trilling, Lionel 23–4

Vietnam War, the 35–6, 100–114

Wallace, Henry 8
Warren Commission, the 110–11
West, Nathanael, *Miss Lonelyhearts* 11
'White Negro, The' 6, 15, 20–1, 23, 25, 27, 29, 64, 80
Whitman, Walt 37–8
Why Are We In Vietnam? 28, 35, 36, 82, 91–2, **100–14**
  allegory in 102–3, 106, 111
  critical views of 101–4, 109
  point-of-view in 108–10
  postmodernism of 107–8
  style of 110
  theology of 111–12